Myths, Legends & Tales

Phyllis J. Perry

Alleyside Press.

Fort Atkinson, Wisconsin

7731508

Published by Alleyside Press,
an imprint of Highsmith Press LLC
Highsmith Press
W5527 Highway 106
P.O. Box 800
Fort Atkinson, Wisconsin 53538-0800
1-800-558-2110

© Copyright by Phyllis J. Perry, 1999
Cover design: Frank Neu

The paper used in this publication meets the minimum requirements of American
National Standard for Information Science — Permanence of Paper for Printed
Library Material. ANSI/NISO Z39.48-1992.

Library of Congress Cataloging in Publication

Perry, Phyllis Jean.
    Myths, legends & tales / Phyllis J. Perry.
        p. cm.
    Includes bibliographical references and index.
    ISBN 1-57950-017-X (pbk. : alk. paper)
    1. Mythology--Juvenile literature--Bibliography. 2. Legends--
Juvenile literature--Bibliography. 3. Mythology--Study and teaching
(Elementary) 4. Legends--Study and teaching (Elementary)
I. Title. II. Title: Myths, legends, and tales.
Z7836.P47 1999
[BL311]
016.3982--dc21   98-48773
                                                                       CIP

For

*teachers, librarians, and media specialists
everywhere,*

*and especially to staff members at the
George Reynolds Branch Library in Boulder, Colorado
who give so generously of their time to assist me:*

*Peter Arnold
Jeni Brice
Anne Stackpole-Cuellar*

Icon illustrations used in the interior of
Myths, Legends & Tales
were prepared by
Clare Marie Miller, age 11.

Contents

Folktales from Around the World

Tall Tales

Introduction

The intent of this book is to assist librarians and teachers as they share myths, legends, and tales with elementary grade and middle school students. Such sharing supports the development of young readers.

Literacy demands are increasing in our society and strong achievement in reading is necessary for all students. But the love of books, the development of reading skills, and a life-long interest in reading don't just happen. Certain factors have to be in place to promote these attitudes, skills, and interest.

Selection Criteria

Students must have access to books—all kinds of books to meet the skill levels and interests of a varied student body. *Myths, Legends & Tales* suggests 80 titles over five sections, selected through discussions with children's librarians, that will have wide appeal to readers. Some of these works are serious, and some are funny. Some are lengthy, and others are short. Some are historical, and some are fanciful. Many have attractive illustrations.

If a unit of study is to be undertaken, an adequate number of books must be made available to students. These 80 titles would be a good place to begin when adding to the classroom or school collection. The titles were recommended by experienced children's librarians and were selected because of the excellent reputations of the authors and to provide a range of reading from the primary grades through middle school.

Additional recommended resources are included at the end of each section of the book. Most of these titles are readily available with copyrights in the 1990s, and a few titles are included from the 1980s.

Using the Reading Activities

Students need to be encouraged to value reading. When classroom teachers and librarians work together on activities which develop research skills and which integrate reading with other disciplines, students see the importance of reading in all areas of their school life. There are suggestions on involving parents, caregivers and school specialists in art and music in many of these activities, too.

By pooling resources and integrating lessons, and by involving parents and caregivers where appropriate, it is more likely that sufficient time is allowed for students to assimilate what they read, to discuss it with students and adults, and to connect it with other aspects of their lives. Suggested activities provide opportunities for students to work alone and on teams as they develop and share ideas.

Although it has paramount importance in every elementary school, reading instruction should not end at the fifth grade. It is particularly important at the middle level, where reading is often ignored, that students continue to benefit from skilled reading teachers. These teachers and librarians, supported by active and interested parents, serve as reading role models and continue to help older students acquire needed skills.

Many of the suggested activities in this book seek to bring members of the community into the schools to share their expertise. The public library, as well as the school media center, and any other specialized libraries in the community are considered to be valued resources that can be drawn upon to help support reading activities through advice, consultation and the loan of materials.

All of the factors mentioned above are important to any strong reading program. For the purposes of this book, the resources mentioned are to support a particular part of the reading program, the study of myths, legends and tales.

Although a study of literature is at the heart of this book, any unit of study of this kind, through the suggested multidisciplinary activities, clearly also involves technology, history, geography, and the arts. Attempts have been made to connect the reading materials with mathematics and science, too.

In each section, there are books which are appropriate to primary grade readers, to intermediate grade readers, and to middle school readers. The reading level of each book is suggested and a brief synopsis is given which will allow the teacher or librarian to help determine which books might be a good fit for which students. Data about authors, illustrators, publishers, the date of publication, and the ISBN number is included.

Following the synopsis of each book there are detailed activities. Headings state that these activities need guidance from a librarian, a classroom teacher, a specialist, or from a parent/caregiver. These headings are not meant to be hard and fast rules but are merely suggestions. A classroom teacher might want to do all the activities with a particular class. A librarian might choose to guide a group in an activity that was suggested for parents. A parent with expertise in a particular area might undertake working with a group of students in an activity that was suggested to have librarian guidance.

Some of these activities might be assigned to a single student, others to a pair of students, and some to small and large groups of students.

The products of student research and creativity might be displayed in the library or the classroom. Some of the activities will take students into other classrooms in the school building or even out into the community.

Teachers, librarians, and parents will have many ideas of their own which might be used in addition to, or in place of, those which are suggested in this book. Students will also come up with unique activities. Resources will grow and change as some Web sites disappear and others are added and as new books are published. This book therefore serves as a springboard rather than a rigid set of guidelines.

How This Book Is Organized

Part One of the book is devoted to Greek Myths. The ancient Greeks invented stories to account for things that happened in the world around them. These stories about various gods and goddesses, called myths, were created by several Greek and Latin poets.

Many of the more famous myths were invented or retold by the Latin poet, Ovid, who lived in Rome from 43 B.C. to A.D.18 He derived many of his stories from Homer and other Greek playwrights. Ovid gathered 250 myths in a collection called *Metamorphoses,* a particularly appropriate name, since many of the people, gods, and goddesses change their form in the stories. A list of additional resources is included.

Part Two deals with Myths and Legends from Around the World. Here students are directed to myths and legends from England, India, Russia, Arabia, stories of the Aztecs, Norse myths, and those of native peoples such as the Maori. These myths were used to explain some of the mysteries of nature, and also provided storytellers with wonderful tales which were passed on from one generation to the next. Additional resources are included at the end of this and all other sections in this book.

Part Three focuses on Native American and Early Indian Myths and Tales. Many of these stories come from Native American tribes that lived in all regions of the United States, while others come from the Maritime Provinces, Mexico, and the Amazon.

Part Four is devoted to Folktales from Around the World. Included are stories from the Eskimos, from England, France, Norway, Puerto Rico, China, Korea, Jamaica, and Transylvania. Single stories and collections of tales make up the reading of this section.

Part Five, Tall Tales, is rich in stories about American adventures. Here are river tales, chuck wagon and campfire tales, and legends about such characters as Mike Fink, Davy Crockett and his wife Sally Ann Thunder Ann Whirlwind Crockett. There are wild and wonderful exaggerated stories about the development of our country which certainly aren't found in history books.

In the hands of dedicated teachers and librarians, this book may contribute to a rich and valuable delving into a treasury of *Myths, Legends & Tales.*

Greek Myths: 1

Ariadne, Awake!
By Doris Orgel • Illustrated by Barry Moser

Summary

The prologue explains how Poseidon took revenge on King Minos by causing Queen Pasiphae to fall in love with a white bull and give birth to a creature with a human body and the head of a bull. This minotaur, who devoured fourteen Athenians yearly, was secretly kept in a maze built by Daedalus.

As the story beings, ten-year-old Ariadne decides to go into the maze and see her half-brother. The minotaur attacks. A keeper appears, and saves her. The next day, Ariadne is summoned to her father and punished.

Years later, when the Athenian youths are brought to be fed to the minotaur, Theseus, a prince who is favored by the god Poseidon, is among them. King Minos throws his ring into the sea and dares Theseus to get it back for him. Theseus returns the ring and a golden head band which he gives to Ariadne.

Ariadne asks Daedalus to help save Theseus. She ties the end of a spool of thread to Theseus's finger before he enters the maze. After he slays the minotaur, Theseus takes Ariadne away in a ship. When she awakes, she finds herself abandoned on an island where a satyr teaches her to dance. Shortly thereafter, Dionysus, a god, returns to the island and marries Ariadne. They live happily, teaching people about grapes and making wine.

Viking, 1994. 74 pp. Watercolor illustrations. ISBN 0-670-85158-2

Activities

With Librarian Guidance

In *Ariadne, Awake!* the minotaur is kept in a maze. Students may be interested in constructing mazes of their own. Refer a group of students to: **http://www.crystalinks.com/mazes.html**. They will find basic information about labyrinths and mazes, and by choosing "Mazes and Labyrinths...how to build a labyrinth" will receive information for a class activity using nesting segments on the number line. *Tony Phillips, Math Dept., SUNY Stony Brook, (http://www.math.sun-ysb.edu/~tony/mazes) created this activity.*

With Classroom Teacher Guidance:

The satyr explains that the young island god was captured by pirates. When Dionysus returns, Ariadne first sees him as a lion. Invite students to write a new chapter for this book in which Dionysus tells of his adventures before returning to Naxos. The adventures should fit with the general setting and characters already presented. Bind the new chapters into a classroom book.

With Parent/Caregiver Guidance

The librarian or classroom teacher might duplicate the summary of the book and a letter like this one to parents:

Dear Parent: Today your child read Ariadne, Awake! *A summary is attached. In the book there were several actions taken by Theseus that reflect on current values. Reasons for the actions of Theseus are given in the epilogue. Your child may wish to learn your opinion regarding his actions. We suggest you read this book with your child, and discuss why Theseus acted as he did.*

Atalanta's Race: A Greek Myth

Retold by Shirley Climo • Illustrated by Alexander Koshkin

Summary

Ancient Greeks told this story for hundreds of years before it was recorded in the first century by the Roman poet Ovid.

King Iasus begs the gods for a son to inherit his kingdom of Arcadia. But when a daughter, Atalanta, is born, the king banishes her to a mountain top. Left in the mouth of a cave, Atalanta is cared for by a bear. In the spring, Ciron, a hunter finds Atalanta, takes her home, and raises her.

When she is fifteen, Atalanta journeys to Athens, Sparta, Corinth, and Olympia. Although females are excluded from the Olympic games, Atalanta wins fame for her speed in foot races. King Iasus summons her and tells her about her birth.

Atalanta remains with the king who hopes for a grandson one day. Atalanta turns away many suitors but agrees to marry any man who can outrun her. The penalty for defeat is death. Many try and lose. Then Melanion, who loves Atalanta, decides to race her. The night before the race, Aphrodite brings him three golden apples which she says will help him win the race.

Melanion diverts Atalanta's attention with the apples, wins the race, and marries Atalanta. The two live happily until Aphrodite complains that Atalanta and Melanion did not thank her for the apples. They are then changed into a lioness and a lion.

Clarion, 1995. 32 pp. Color illustrations. ISBN 0-395-67322-4

Activities

With Librarian Guidance

Atalanta's Race provides a springboard for researching the Olympic Games. Many references are available, such as G.B. Hennesey's **Olympics!** (Viking, 1996) and an interactive multimedia CD **Olympic Gold: A 100 Year History of the Summer Olympic Games,** (S.R.B. Multimedia: Bethesda, MD: Discovery Communication, 1995, 1 computer laser optical disc). Make available all the appropriate materials you have and encourage students to use the *Reader's Guide* to locate other materials.

1. Using available reference materials, ask a pair of students to research some of the women's short dashes in the last Olympic Games. On a chart, show the distances, who won the three medals, and which countries they represented.

2. Invite another pair of students to research the women's long races in the last Olympic Games. On a chart, show the distances, names of winners, and the countries they represented.

With Parent/Caregiver Guidance

The librarian or classroom teacher might reprint the summary of the book and this letter.

Dear Parent: Your child has read Atalanta's Race *in which King Iasus begs the gods for a son to rule after him. However, many women have been very successful leaders. Discuss this with your child and ask him or her to name some successful women such as Queen Victoria and Margaret Thatcher. You may visit the library and select some books to share with your child and then discuss these women's achievements.*

Black Ships Before Troy
The Story of the Iliad
By Rosemary Sutcliff • Illustrated by Alan Lee

Summary

Sutcliff retells Homer's epic poem, *The Iliad*, using the most current research on ancient Greece and Troy. She has divided the book into nineteen sections: "The Golden Apple, Ship-gathering, Quarrel with the High King, Single Combat, The Women of Troy, The High King's Embassy, The Horses of King Rhesus, Red Rain, Battle for the Ships, The Armor of Achilles, Vengeance for Patroclus, Funeral Games, Ransom for Hector, The Luck of Troy, Warrior Women, The Death of Achilles, Poisoned Arrow, The Wooden Horse," and "The Fall of Troy." There is also a final section on pronunciation followed by a listing of source books.

The author begins with the golden apple brought by Eris to the wedding of Peleus and Thetis. From this beginning, the rest of the tale follows: Paris awards the apple to Aphrodite, Helen is stolen by Paris, the black ships set out, there is combat between armies and individuals, gods intervene, there are burials of great princes on both sides, the Luck of Troy is stolen, the Amazons and Ethiopians appear, Achilles is killed by Paris's arrow, Ajax commits suicide, a poisoned arrow kills Paris, the wooden horse is brought into the very heart of Troy, Cassandra gives warning, the Greek ships pretend to retreat, Troy is burned, and finally Helen is saved by Odysseus.

Delacorte, 1993. 128 pp. Watercolors illustrations. ISBN 0-385-31069-2

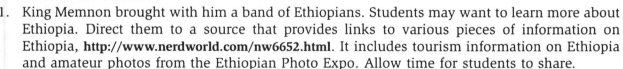

Activities

With Librarian Guidance

1. King Memnon brought with him a band of Ethiopians. Students may want to learn more about Ethiopia. Direct them to a source that provides links to various pieces of information on Ethiopia, **http://www.nerdworld.com/nw6652.html**. It includes tourism information on Ethiopia and amateur photos from the Ethiopian Photo Expo. Allow time for students to share.

2. Have students research the geographic location of ancient Troy using a standard historical atlas such as **The Times Atlas of World History**, edited by Geoffrey Barraclough (Hammond, 1993) or other available historical atlas.

With Classroom Teacher Guidance

Some students in class would enjoy a book discussion group formed around reading Clemence McClaren's **Inside the Walls of Troy: A Novel of the Women Who lived the Trojan War** (Atheneum, 1996, 199 pp.).

With Parent/Caregiver Guidance

The librarian or classroom teacher might duplicate the summary of this book and the following letter:

Dear Parent: Your child read Black Ships Before Troy. *There are many interpretations about the meaning of the image of the Trojan Horse. The Reader's Advisory, Encarta Encyclopedia and the Web site http://www.homer.edu all provide some answers. However, talk with your child about what you believe is its meaning. You may want to help your child use these resources to gain insight into other interpretations.*

 *Greek Myths: 4*

Cupid and Psyche

Retold by M. Charlotte Craft • Illustrated by K. Y. Craft

Summary

A king and queen have three daughters. Two marry kings, but the youngest daughter, Psyche, is so beautiful that no one dares asks her to marry. Jealous Venus sends Cupid to shoot an arrow to cause Psyche to fall in love with a frightening creature. But when Cupid reaches her bed chamber, Psyche startles him and he nicks himself with an arrow and falls in love. An oracle tells Psyche she will marry someone feared by the gods. Zephyrus, the gentle wind, carries Psyche to a distant valley where she sees a beautiful palace and is joined by an unseen companion.

Psyche's sisters persuade her to steal a look at her host, and that night, by lantern light she does. Psyche pricks herself with Cupid's arrow and falls in love with him, but Cupid leaves.

Venus sets three tasks for Psyche to complete to be reunited with Cupid. Ants help her separate barley, wheat and millet. A sparrow gives her advice on how to bring home the golden fleece. The last task requires her to visit Proserpine in the underworld. Psyche completes her journey, but she opens the box of beauty and finds instead the sleep of the dead. Cupid comes, removes the sleep and puts it back in the box, and Psyche awakes.

Jupiter gives Psyche a cup of ambrosia making her immortal. Cupid and Psyche wed and have a daughter whom they name Joy.

William Morrow, 1996. 40 pp. Extensive illustrations. ISBN 0-688-13163-8

Activities

With Librarian Guidance

Cupid has long been associated with Valentine's Day. *Chase's Calendar of Events* (Contemporary Books, annual) identifies a variety of special events and other notable occasions. Using *Chase's Calendar* or a similar book, find out how Cupid became associated with Valentine's Day. What other events took place on February 14? Look up your birthday and identify who else was born on that date. Can your think of other ways this book can help you in the future?

With Classroom Teacher Guidance

There are many versions of myths. After students have read *Cupid and Psyche*, they may enjoy looking at **http://209.1/.224.12/Athens/Forum/6946/myths.html.** This site, Back to the Forum, provides versions of Greek myths. Ask students to read the version there of *Cupid and Psyche* and to write down any differences they find between it and the Craft book.

With Parent/Caregiver Guidance

The librarian or classroom teacher might duplicate the summary of Psyche and Cupid and the following letter:

Dear Parent: Your child has read Psyche and Cupid *(summary attached) and is being asked to write a paragraph comparing Psyche and Cupid with Echo and Narcissus. Books containing these myths and recordings of the myths on audiotape are available for check-out in the library. You may want to visit the library to examine and check out these materials and then discuss with your child how these two pairs are alike and different.*

Cyclops

Written and illustrated by Leonard Everett Fisher

Summary

As the story begins, Odysseus and his men are sailing home to Ithaca after the long Trojan War. The gods are angry at the warriors for not respecting a temple in Troy, so they send a fierce storm that batters the ship and blows it off course.

Odysseus and his men land on the shore of an island. Odysseus takes twelve men to search for food. They find a well-stocked cave. While they are eating, the owner of the cave, a giant, one-eyed cyclops, returns with a herd of sheep.

The giant comes inside the cave and moves a great boulder in front of the opening. The giant tells them he is Polyphemus, then reaches out, picks up two of the Greeks and eats them before falling asleep in the cave. In the morning, Polyphemus eats two more men. Then, accompanied by his sheep, he leaves, covering the entrance again with the boulder.

When he returns, Odysseus offers him wine, telling the giant his name is Noman. The giant drinks the wine, and while he is asleep, Odysseus and his men blind the giant with a sharpened stake. In the morning, when Polyphemus lets the sheep out, the men, strapped beneath the sheep, are able to escape. They rush to the sea, avoid being swamped by a boulder Polyphemus throws, and sail away leaving behind the giant who was injured by Noman.

Holiday House, 1991. 32 pp. Full-color, dramatic illustrations. ISBN 0-8234-0891-4

Activities

With Librarian Guidance

The book opens with a map that shows the location of the island of Sicily where the Cyclops lived. Ask a pair of students to research modern Sicily. They should use the library's card or electronic catalog to locate appropriate books. What is Sicily like today in terms of its agriculture, climate, cities, and government? Ask the students to write a short report on what they learn, including a bibliography, to share the highlights with the class orally, and to post the report on a bulletin board or on a school Web site.

With Classroom Teacher Guidance

Students might enjoy presenting this story as a puppet show. Using a tape recorder, a narrator can be used to describe the opening storm at sea and the escape. Stick puppets can be used to show the adventures in the cave. Sound effects such as the sheep bleating, the storm, etc., can be tape recorded. The final piece might be shared with another class.

With Parent/Caregiver Guidance

The librarian or classroom teacher might duplicate the summary of the book and the following letter:

Dear Parent: Your child has read Cyclops *(summary attached). Not satisfied with his cleverness, Odysseus couldn't resist taunting the giant. His actions almost caused the death of his men. Your child might want to hear your opinions on this. Does "having the last word" sometimes cause trouble? How could Odysseus have acted more wisely?*

Favorite Greek Myths

Retold by Mary Pope Osborne • Illustrated by Troy Howell

Summary

"Chariot of the Sun God" tells how Phaeton begs his father, Helios, to allow him to drive the fiery chariot of the sun across the sky. In "The Golden Touch," King Midas asks Bacchus to grant the golden touch. "Lost at Sea," tells the story of Ceyx and Alcyone. When Ceyx drowns at sea and his body comes to shore, Alcyone, in the form of a bird, rushes to greet him. He, too, changes into a bird, and the two are together again.

In "The Weaving Contest," Arachne is changed into a spider by the jealous and angry goddess, Minerva. "Apollo's Tree," tells the story of how Cupid's arrows affected Daphne and Apollo. "The Face in the Pool" explains why Echo has the last word, but never the first, and how Narcissus loves only his reflection in the pool. "The Kidnapping," tells how Pluto takes Proserpina away from her mother, Ceres, to live with him in the underworld but is forced to return her for six months of the year.

The story of Callisto and Arcus is told in "The Great Bear." In "Journey to the Underworld," the reader learns how Orpheus lost Eurydice to the land of the dead. "The Golden Apples," tells how Hippomenes wins Atalanta's hand in marriage. Cupid and Psyche are the subjects of "The Four Tasks," and "The Mysterious Visitors," tells of generous Baucis and Philemon.

Scholastic, 1989. 81 pp. Full-color illustrations. ISBN 0-590-41339-2

Activities

With Librarian Guidance

Morpheus is the god of dreams. Invite a pair of interested students to research morphine, a drug used to alleviate pain. How is it made? How does it work? If available, direct the students to **The Merck Index: An Encyclopedia of Chemicals & Drugs** (Merck, 1996). After initial research, the students might want to make an appointment with a willing local physician for follow-up questions. Allow time for students to share what they learn.

With Classroom Teacher Guidance

Cereal, a breakfast food of grains, gets its name from Ceres, goddess of grains. Encourage a small group of students to write a 30-second television spot to persuade the public to buy a certain cereal. The students might include a "jingle" to be sung and an "illustration" to appear on the cereal box, as well as a brief announcement. Somewhere in the spot announcement, Ceres should be featured. Allow time for the students to present their spot announcement to the class.

With Parent/Care Giver Guidance

The librarian or classroom teacher might prepare a letter like this for parents:

Dear Parent: Your child has read Favorite Greek Myths *(summary attached). During this unit on Greek mythology, it would be helpful if students could list the information given about the various gods in a chart format for ready reference. We suggest you read this book with your child and discuss the information that would be appropriate for inclusion in a chart.*

The Gods and Goddesses of Olympus

By Aliki

Summary

The book begins with an explanation of how people in ancient Greece began telling myths in an attempt to explain the mysteries of life and death. These myths were about heroes, monsters, gods, and goddesses. The mightiest of these immortal gods lived on Mount Olympus, but whenever they wished, gods could adopt any shape and come and live on earth. People built temples to honor these gods.

The next section of the book offers an explanation of how Gaea, the Earth, grew out of Chaos, gave birth to the sky, and became the mother of all living things. Gaea and Uranus are parents of Titans and monsters. Uranus banishes the monsters, and Gaea urges Cronus to dethrone his father. Cronus marries Rhea, and swallows his own children. Rhea manages to hide her baby, Zeus, who succeeds in defeating Cronus and the Titans and banishes them to the underworld. Zeus rules heaven and earth, Poseidon is god of the sea, and Hades rules the underworld. The Cyclopes build a palace, and Zeus shares it with his brothers and sisters, six of his children, and Aphrodite, the goddess of love. The remainder of the book devotes a short section to each of the Olympians: Zeus, Hera, Hephaestus, Aphrodite with Eros, Ares, Poseidon, Athena, Hermes, Artemis, Apollo, Hades, Demeter with Persephone, Dionysus, and Hestia.

HarperCollins, 1994. 48 pp. Full-color illustrations. ISBN 0-06-023530-6

Activities

With Librarian Guidance

Hestia kept the Olympic flame burning. Invite a pair of students to research the Olympic flame at the many Web sites that are available. They will find information about the ancient games at **http://www.netaxis.qc.ca/people/a.tzouvelakos/Olympic/index.html**.

If they visit **http://www.torchrun.com/torchpr/html**, they can learn how the 1996 torch was made, and they can print out a copy of a map which traces the relay route for the 1996 games involving 10,000 torchbearers across 15,000 miles from Los Angeles to Atlanta.

With Classroom Teacher Guidance

Hermes made a lyre. A group of students might want to make simple stringed instruments. The rate that something vibrates determines the sound that it makes. Stretch three rubber bands around a sturdy cardboard box that is about two inches deep and eight inches square. Pluck the bands. Now stretch a band tighter, and tie a knot to shorten it. Does the sound change?

With Parent/Care Giver Guidance

The librarian or classroom teacher might send a letter like this to parents:

Dear Parent: Students have read The Gods and Goddesses of Olympus *(summary attached) and are being asked to write a short paper about a new Olympian. Your child may wish to learn your opinion about what god or goddess might be added to sit on Olympus. We suggest you read this book with your child and discuss the special characteristics this new Olympian might have and in what area this god or goddess would take special interest.*

The Hydra
By Bernard Evslin

Summary

As the book begins, the reader learns that the four winds are children of the Titan, Astraeus, and the dawn goddess, Eos. Boreas, in the north, Notus in the south, and Euros on the east, all love Iris, the rainbow goddess. Boreas plans to kidnap her.

Young Hercules visits a beautiful meadow where nymphs make dyes for the rainbow goddess, Iris. One day, Hercules finds the nymphs crying because Iris has been kidnapped by Boreas.

Hercules sets off to rescue her. Boreas is protected by an array of beasts and demons. Hercules dives into the water, and is covered in an armor of ice. He fights off wolves, polar bears, frost demons, and owls. When Boreas approaches, Hercules knocks him down and rescues Iris. Iris's daughter, Iole, loves to hear her mother tell the story of her rescue, and Iole hopes to meet Hercules one day.

Zeus orders that anyone killing a relative must spend a year serving the family. Hera deflects one of Hercules' arrows so that a prince is killed, and Hercules must serve the king of Mycenae. Iole goes to help Hercules. Hercules is sent to slay the Nemean lion. Then he is sent to kill the many-headed hydra. With Iole's help, Hercules succeeds in both his tasks.

It is one of the Monsters of Mythology series.

Chelsea House, 1989. 77 pp. Full-color illustrations. ISBN 1-555-46253-7

Activities

With Librarian Guidance

According to the story, Iris's frozen rainbow burns about the North Wind's castle and is called the Northern Lights. Invite a pair of students to research this topic and write a short paper with a bibliography to share with the class. Ask the students to locate and use three different types of resources in researching their paper, such as an encyclopedia, a Web site, a specialized reference book, a nonfiction book, or a magazine or journal. Students should learn the answers to the following questions: What are the Northern Lights? What causes them? When are they visible?

With Classroom Teacher Guidance

It is likely that Notus and Euros will want to get even with their brother, Boreas, for the destruction he brought on them. Ask interested students to write an original short story in which the winds plot to get even. Zephyrus might also be in the story. Bind the completed short stories into a class book.

With Parent/Care Taker Guidance

The librarian or classroom teacher might send home the following letter:

Dear Parent: Your child has read The Hydra *(summary attached). Hera tries unsuccessfully to kill Iole by sending a giant crab after her. Hera names the crab Cancer and puts it in the sky. Many books on constellations are available in the school and local library. Research one with your child so that he or she can make a map of the sky showing where Cancer can be found.*

Jason and the Golden Fleece

Retold and illustrated by Leonard Everett Fisher

Summary

Jason's father should have been king of Iolcos, but the country is ruled instead by a wicked cousin named Pelias. When Jason demands the throne, Pelias says he will give the kingdom back if Jason brings him the golden fleece which hangs in a sacred grove in Colechis.

Jason sets off in the ship, Argo, and lands on the island of Lemnos where the women have killed all the men but the old king. Here they lose two men to a sea nymph. On another island, they meet and help Phineus, who warns them of dangers ahead, telling them how to safely slip between two crushing rocks at Symplegades and advising them to avoid the land of the Amazons.

In Colechis, the king sets four tasks which Jason must complete to have the fleece: yoke two fire-breathing bulls, plow a field, sow the furrows with dragon teeth, and defeat an army alone. The king's daughter, Medea, helps him, and Jason succeeds in these tasks and in taking the golden fleece from the dragon.

Jason sails home with the fleece only to find his parents dead. Again, with Medea's help, Pelias is murdered. Jason and Medea flee to Corinth where they marry and have children. When Jason falls in love with Glauce, daughter of the King of Corinth, he banishes Medea. In revenge, she destroys Glauce, and her own children, then escapes, leaving Jason to roam Greece alone.

Holiday House, 1990. 32pp. Full-color illustrations. ISBN 0-8234-0794-2

Activities

With Librarian Guidance

Phineas almost starved because of the Harpies. Invite a pair of students to research and photocopy (with permission) or sketch pictures of the following: Harpy eagle, golden eagle, imperial eagle, bald eagle, and sea eagle. To carry out this task, students need access to different resources. Field guides such as ***The Audubon Society Master Guide to Birding*** (Knopf, 1983) or the ***Audubon Field Guide*** (Audubon Society, 1994) would be helpful, as well as nonfiction books such as ***Birds of Prey***, by Malcolm Penny (Thomson Learning, 1996), ***Eagles***, by Casey Horton (Marshall Cavendish, 1996), and ***Hawks & Eagles***, by George K. Peck (Smart Apple, 1997).

With Classroom Teacher Guidance

The dragon in this book, under a spell from Medea, does no harm to Jason. Students may have met dragons, both fierce and friendly, in other books. Ask the class to write dragon poems and to include an illustration. Bind the poems together into a class book of "Dragon Poetry."

With Parent/Care Giver Guidance

The librarian or classroom teacher should photocopy (with permission) the opening map in the book and send it home to parents with the following letter.

Dear Parent: Your child has read Jason and the Golden Fleece *(summary and map attached). You may wish to read this book with your child and use the attached blank map to identify and locate the sites of Jason's various adventures. Your child should mark the spots mentioned in the story on the map and keep it for future reference during this unit on Greek myths.*

Ladon

By Bernard Evslin

Summary

Ladon, an enormous sea serpent, crawls out of the sea and acquires a taste for humans. Hera, Queen of the Gods, has an ongoing quarrel with Hercules, and she decides to use Ladon against Hercules since her recent attempts to kill him have failed.

Hecate journeys to the upper regions to tell Hera that Iris or Iris's daughter, Iole, must be helping Hercules. Fearing Hera, Iris and Iole go into hiding. Iole searches for Hercules and comes upon Ladon who falls in love with her. She tells him she could never marry a creature who eats people, so Ladon promises to change and begins eating crops.

Ares, God of War, sends Hypnos with a dream to one of the Amazons, Thyone, who goes out, finds a poet on Helicon and marries him. When the Amazon queen learns of this, she sets out for Helicon. Fearing for the poets, Hypnos sends Hercules to protect them. Iole learns that Hercules is on Helicon and gets Ladon to bring her there. Hercules chases a stag. While Iole sleeps, Ladon sets after Hercules to kill him. When they reach an island, Ladon eats the stag. Hercules finds the bloody antlers and stabs Ladon. Hercules rafts back from the island, and Iole rushes to meet him.

This book is part of Chelsea House's Monsters of Mythology series.

Chelsea House, 1990. 88 pp. Color photographs. ISBN 1-555-46254-5

Activities

With Librarian Guidance

1. Ladon is a sea serpent who crawls on land. Without legs, snakes can move across the ground. Students may be interested in learning how snakes use friction to move. There is an excellent lesson at **http://192.156.97.132/kn/itv/snake.sht**. It provides learning objectives, a list of simple materials, previewing and post-viewing activities, an action plan, and extensions. The lesson, Snakes & Skates, is appropriate for middle level students and was prepared as part of the 1996-97 National Teacher Training Institute.

2. Chased by Hercules, the stag leaps into the English Channel and swims across it. Several people in modern times have also set records by attempting to swim the Channel. Ask a pair of students to use the *Reader's Guide to Periodical Literature* to locate articles about channel swimmers. Have them make a list of articles and try to locate a copy of one or more of them through interlibrary loan for the students to read.

With Classroom Teacher Guidance

Many families have family portraits taken. Ladon's "family portrait" would be very interesting. Invite seven students to draw pictures and group the finished drawings to make a composite family portrait. Include Ladon, his sister Echidne, her son the dog Cerberus, a cousin Polypus, Ladon's niece, the Sphinx, and Ladon's parents, Ceto and Phorcys. Post the composite family portrait on a classroom bulletin board.

Persephone

Retold and illustrated by Warwick Hutton

Summary

Zeus ruled the heavens and the earth, Poseidon was god of the seas, and the underworld was ruled by Hades. In his dark world, Hades could find no one who would marry him. One day as Hades wandered on the earth in a chariot looking for a queen, he saw Persephone, the daughter of the goddess Demeter.

Hades carried Persephone off in his chariot. When he got to the river Cyane, a large wave formed to threaten the chariot. But Hades struck open the earth and disappeared with Persephone.

Demeter, the goddess of growing things, looked for her daughter day after day, ignoring her duties. Below the earth, Persephone cried. Hades showed her his grove of pomegranates which only made Persephone miss her mother more.

One day Demeter walked to a bubbling spring that told her where her daughter was. Zeus sent the messenger, Hermes, to Hades saying that if Persephone had eaten nothing since she had been kidnapped, she must be returned to her mother.

Because she had eaten six pomegranate seeds, Zeus ruled that Persephone must spend six months a year with Hades and could spend the other six with her mother. Since then, the earth has spring and summer when Persephone is with her mother and fall and winter when she is with Hades.

M. K. McElderry, 1994. 32 pp. Watercolor illustrations. ISBN 0 689-50600-7

Activities

With Librarian Guidance

To provide second and third graders with an introduction to finding information on the Web, have them visit: **http://www.dinersgrapevine.com/palisade/lordbromios/artemis/styx.htm.** They will find information about the Rivers Styx, Lethe, Phlegethon, Cocytus, and Acheron. Let the group decide how to present this information to the class.

With Classroom Teacher Guidance

This story in an imaginative way accounts for the seasons of the year. What really causes earth's seasons? Why is it summer on one part of the earth at the same time that another part of the earth is having winter? Ask a small group of students to research this topic and to prepare diagrams or charts or use a model to show what happens to our planet with respect to the sun which causes our seasons. Have the students present their explanation to the class in an oral report.

With Parent/Caregiver Guidance

The librarian might duplicate the summary of the book and a letter like this to parents:

Dear Parent: Your child has read Persephone *(summary attached). The book explains seasons of the year. Many seasonal poems have been written. With your child, read and discuss some seasonal poetry from collections in your home, school, or public library. Help your child pick out a favorite and copy it on a sheet of paper to go on a SEASONS library bulletin board. (Be sure to include the poet's name.)*

The Robber Baby
Stories from the Greek Myths
Retold and illustrated by Anne Rockwell

Summary

Fourteen myths are included: "The Robber Baby" explains how Hermes became the messenger of the gods. "The Mother Who Lost Her Daughter" tells how Hades rose up from the underworld and kidnapped Persephone to be his wife. In "The Hero and His Horse," Bellerophon performs great feats on the winged horse Pegasus before being exiled for his conceit.

"The Four Winds," explains how Zeus appointed Aeolus as the keeper of all the winds. The story of Hephaestus and his many tools and inventions is told in "The Cruel Mother." "The Boy Who Flew" explains how Daedalus, and his son, Icarus, came to be imprisoned in a tower on the island of Crete. "The Girl Who Won All the Races" tells how Hippomenes beat Atalanta in a race. "Pandora's Box" shows how curiosity was Pandora's undoing. The story of Orpheus and Eurydice is related in "The Bride Who Stepped On a Snake." The reader learns about Echo in "The Nymph Who Had the Last Word." The story of how Artemis turned Actaeon into a stag is related in "The Hunter and His Hounds." In "The God Who Was Kidnapped by Pirates," Dionysus turns a ships' crew into dolphins. The story of Midas and his golden touch is related in "The King Who Wished for Gold," and the birth of Pan is described in "The Goat-Footed God."

Greenwillow, 1994. 80 pp. Serigraphs, hand-painted with watercolors. ISBN 0-688-09741-3

Activities

With Librarian Guidance

In the story "The Boy Who Flew," Daedalus manages to fly. Invite a group of students to research people who contributed to flight. They should use the Internet, an encyclopedia, magazines, nonfiction books, and any available specialized references such as *Eureka!*, a six-volume set (Thompson, 1995), that documents inventions and discoveries. They should choose their topic from the following list, and write a short report to be posted on the bulletin board or on a school Web site: Robert Kronfeld, Leonardo da Vinci, Jean Marie Le Bris, the Schweizer brothers, Otto Lillienthal, Alexander Lippisch, Louis Pierre Mouillard, Matthew Bacon Sellers, and the Wright brothers.

With Classroom Teacher Guidance

The artist did not provide a picture of Triptolemus for page 22. However, there is an excellent description. He was the older brother of a swineherd, and he had a chariot pulled by dragons. Invite students to make their own illustrations and post these on a classroom bulletin board.

With Classroom Teacher/Parent Volunteer Guidance

"The King Who Wished for Gold" could be presented as a short play. Invite interested parent volunteers to work with a drama group. They might rehearse during class time, during the noon hour, or before or after school depending on schedules. Students should study the play, rehearse, and perform it before the class using simple costumes and props.

Scylla and Charybdis

By Bernard Evslin

Summary

As the story begins, Scylla, an infant abandoned during a rock slide, is raised by wolves. Scylla learns she is destined to stalk the son of the Hawk. In Egypt, Nisus, a prince descended from the Hawk, is born. The beast gods, Buto and Bast, are his enemies. Nisus sails from Egypt, and following advice from Thoth, steals some cattle from King Minos of Crete.

Scylla comes upon Nisus in Corinth. He flies, and because she loves flying, Scylla marries him. Scylla is restless and one night runs with the wolves and attacks the cattle. Nisus organizes a wolf hunt and to Scylla's horror, kills them.

Minos attacks Corinth. Buto and Bast convince King Minos to change into a wolf to woo Scylla. Scylla is abandoned by Minos and changed by Poseidon into a nymph. Then his wife changes Scylla into a monster that is a nymph on the top half of her body but has six wolf heads below.

For angering Demeter, Charybdis, a princess, is turned into a hungry monster and placed just opposite Scylla where she acts as a whirlpool. It is between Scylla and Charybdis that Ulysses is forced to sail on his return home after the Trojan War, losing four men to Scylla.

Chelsea House, 1989. 100 pp. Color photographs. ISBN 1-55546-257-X

Activities

With Librarian Guidance

Several books have been written about the interaction between humans and wolves. Ask a pair of students to use a computerized public access catalog to prepare a list of books that others might enjoy reading about humans and wolves. Include title, author, publisher, and date. Post the list on a bulletin board and assist interested students in borrowing copies through interlibrary loan.

With Classroom Teacher Guidance

In addition to the monsters Scylla and Charybdis, there are many other famous monsters in mythology. From the following list, have interested students choose a topic for research: Amycus, Antcus, Cerberus, Chimaera, Cyclopes, Hecate, Hydra, Minotaur, Procrustes, and Medusa. They should draw a picture of the monster they select and write a one-page paper telling about the monster. Bind the pictures and reports into a class book.

With Parent/Caregiver Guidance

The classroom teacher or librarian might prepare the following note to be sent home:

Dear Parent: Your child has read Scylla and Charybdis *(summary attached) which contains several complex words. Your child is being asked to write definitions for these words: waif, pauperized, loathing, essence, flayed, phlegmy, palisade, decapitation, insignia, thwarted, emaciated, mandate, paeans, and halcyon. Your child might want to locate these words in the book and discuss with you which definition fits the context.*

The Trojan Horse

Retold and illustrated by Warwick Hutton

Summary

This is the ancient tale of how Helen, the beautiful young wife of King Menelaus of Sparta, meets and falls in love with Paris, the son of King Priam of Troy. When Helen sails away with Paris, Menelaus gathers an army of Greeks to sail after them and destroy the city of Troy.

The battle between these armies goes on for ten years with first one side and then the other seeming to have the advantage. Then one day, the Greeks close their camps, climb back into their ships and sail away. The Trojans think that their enemies have given up and sailed home.

But the Greeks left a giant wooden horse behind on the beach. One of the Trojan high priests warns his countrymen about this horse. But a Greek spy tells them the Greeks fear that the Trojans will drag the horse into the city by enlarging its gates; this would please Athena, and she would favor them. The Trojans drag the horse into their city. Late that night, the Greeks, hidden in the belly of the horse, come out and are joined by the Greek armies who have sailed back to Troy in the darkness. They take the city.

The Greek soldiers kill their enemies, take treasures from the city, capture prisoners, and finally burn the city of Troy to the ground before sailing home in victory.

M. K. McElderry, 1992. 32 pp. Illustrations with watercolors and pen. ISBN 0 689-50542-6

Activities

With Librarian Guidance

Primary grade students may want to check into Crayola Kids Adventures: "The Trojan Horse," to learn more about the war and see pictures and scenes from a movie on the topic. They should visit **http://www.crayola.com/cka/trojan/2.html.** They will also find a game there to play about something that's hidden in Troy. Students may make their own game based on the story of the Trojan Horse. They might, for example, make a pack of cards showing characters from the story, along with their names and play it like "Go Fish." Or they may adapt a game from *500 Five Minute Games*, by Jackie Silberg (Gryphon House, 1995) or a similar game book.

With Classroom Teacher Guidance

The Trojans came down on the beach to look at the horse because they were curious. Curiosity often causes people to get in trouble. Invite students to write original short stories in which a character's curiosity brings about problems. Allow time for those who wish to read their stories to the class.

With Parent/Caregiver Guidance

Students might wish to make a miniature papier-mâché Trojan Horse for the classroom. The librarian might put out a call for adult volunteers to help the students make the basic structure of the horse using chicken wire. Then papier-mâché strips (torn newspaper or paper towels) can be applied with thin wallpaper paste in several coats. Finally the horse can be painted and decorated and put on display in the media center.

The Wanderings of Odysseus
The Story of the Odyssey
By Rosemary Sutcliff • Illustrated by Alan Lee

Summary

This book follows Odysseus after he leaves Troy and heads back to Ithaca after the long Trojan War. The book is divided into the following sections: "Prologue, The Sacker of Cities, The Cyclops, The Lord of the Winds, The Enchantress, The Land of the Dead, Sea Perils, Telemachus Seeks His Father, Farewell to Calypso, The King's Daughter, The Phaeacian Games, Return to Ithaca, The Beggar in the Corner, The Archery Contest, The Slaying of the Suitors," and "Peace in the Islands." A map and pronunciation guide complete the book.

As Odysseus sails for home, he finds that the return voyage holds more hazards than he faced during the war. An ill wind forces him into unknown seas. First he visits the coast of Thrace, sacks the city, and loses 70 of his men. Then he visits the land of the lotus eaters and the land of the Cyclops. From Aeolus he receives the gift of all the winds which curious sailors release at the shore of Ithaca and which blow him away on more journeys. Odysseus visits the witch Circe, the land of the dead, the Sirens, Scylla and Charybdis, the cattle of Hyperion, Calypso's island, and Phaecia, before reaching Ithaca.

The final sections describe how Odysseus rejoins his son, wife, and father, and reclaims his kingdom.

Delacorte, 1995. 120 pp. Watercolors illustrations. ISBN 0-385-32205-4

Activities

With Librarian Guidance

Students might wonder what is going on in other areas at the same time as the Trojan War. This would be a good time to introduce **The Timetable of History**, by Bernard Grun (Simon & Schuster, 1991). It provides a horizontal linkage of people and events showing: history/politics; literature/theatre; religion/philosophy/learning; visual arts; music; science/technology/growth; and daily life. Students might then choose another period in history in which they are interested and see what they can learn from *The Timetable*.

With Classroom Teacher Guidance

1. Students who have read both *The Black Ships Before Troy* and *The Wanderings of Odysseus* would benefit from a discussion group. One of the traits of Odysseus is that in addition to being strong and a great warrior, he is a clever and original thinker. Invite students to discuss what evidence they have of the cleverness of Odysseus from reading both books. How many instances of his inventiveness can they find?

2. In this book, there is only a brief mention of Sisyphus rolling a mighty boulder up hill. Invite two students to research and learn more about Sisyphus. Have them keep a detailed list of all the sources of information that they find (print and nonprint). Allow time for the students to orally report to the class what they learn. One Web site that would be helpful to students is **http://www.sisyphuscafe.com/myth/**.

Wings

By Jane Yolen • Illustrated by Dennis Nolan

Summary

Wings tells of Daedalus, a prince of Greece, who lives in Athens. Daedalus is highly respected for his inventions and his art. But he is exiled for causing the death of his nephew.

After traveling for a year and a day, Daedalus arrives in Crete, where he is welcomed by King Minos. The king explains that his wife has given birth to a minotaur, born with a bull's head and a man's body. The king wants Daedalus to build a labyrinth where the minotaur can live, and Daedalus designs the labyrinth for the minotaur. In time, Daedalus marries and has a son named Icarus. One night, a prince of Greece, Theseus, comes and asks Daedalus for help. Daedalus learns that every seven years, Athens sends a tribute of boys and girls to Crete where they are put into the labyrinth and devoured by the minotaur. Daedalus draws a map enabling Theseus to destroy the minotaur.

King Minos then locks Daedalus and Icarus into a tower. The father and son collect feathers from the birds that visit them, and Daedalus fashions wings from these feathers using candle wax and the leather from their sandals. One day, the two fly away from the tower. But Icarus flies too high, the wax melts, and he falls into the sea and drowns. Daedalus flies to Sicily and builds a temple to the god Apollo.

Harcourt Brace Jovanovich, 1991, 32 pp. Full-page watercolor illustrations. ISBN 0-15-297850-X

Activities

With Librarian and Art Educator Guidance

The minotaur is but one of the famous Greek monsters. The librarian should locate as many books as possible in the school library (and through interlibrary loan) with pictures of the various Greek monsters. Share these pictures with the students. With the help of the art educator, have the students plan and design a mural on which they draw and label the names of the different monsters from Greek mythology. Display the completed mural in the library media center.

With Classroom Teacher Guidance

Flight is often of interest to students. Hold a paper airplane contest. Allow anyone who wishes to design and make a paper airplane to enter. On contest day, find a place outside for the airplanes to be flown. An award might be given for the plane that stays up longest or covers the greatest distance. Provide reference books such as Norman Schmidt's **Best Ever Paper Airplanes** (Sterling, 1994).

With Parent/Caregiver Guidance

This myth could make an effective dramatic presentation. Ask interested parents to volunteer to work with the class to present the play. The directors could divide a class into three groups: readers, actors, and a Greek chorus. One student reads a page of text, while students in simple costumes, mime the action. After each scene, the Greek chorus reads the line(s) in italics at the end of each page.

More Resources for Greek Myths

Books

Baker, Charles F. *Myths and Legends of Mount Olympus.* Cobblestone, 1992.

Cassini, Marc A. *The Twelve Labors of Hercules.* Random House, 1997.

Evans, Cheryl. *Greek Myths and Legends.* Usborne Pub., 1986.

Evslin, Bernard. *The Furies.* Chelsea House, 1989.

Geringer, Laura. *Castor & Pollux: The Fighting Twins.* Scholastic, 1997.

———. *Iole: the Girl with Super Powers.* Scholastic, 1997.

———. *Theseus: Hero of the Maze.* Scholastic, 1997.

Hawthorne, Nathaniel. *Wonder Book for Girls & Boys.* Knopf, 1994.

Martin, Claire. *The Race of the Golden Apples.* Dial Books, 1991.

McCaughrean, Geraldine. *Greek Myths.* Margaret E. McElderry, 1993.

Metaxas, Eric. *King Midas & the Golden Touch.* Picture Book Studio, 1992.

Mikolaycak, Charles. *Orpheus.* Harcourt Brace Jovanovich, 1992.

Newham, Paul. *The Outlandish Adventures of Orpheus in the Underworld.* Barefoot, 1994.

Philip, Neil. *The Adventures of Odysseus.* Orchard, 1997.

Rockwell, Anne F. *The One-Eyed Giant and Other Monsters from the Greek Myths.* Greenwillow, 1996.

———. *Romulus and Remus.* Simon & Schuster Books for Young Readers, 1997.

Ross, Stewart. *Gods & Giants.* Copper Beech Books, 1997.

———. *Warriors & Witches.* Copper Beech Books, 1997.

Williams, Marcia. *Greek Myths for Young Children.* Candlewick, 1992.

———. *The Iliad and the Odyssey.* Candlewick, 1996.

Video

King Midas and the Golden Touch. Westport, CT: Rabbit Ears Productions, distributed by UNI Distributing Corporation, 1991. 1 videocassette, 30 min. A retelling of the ancient Greek tale.

Demons, Gods & Holy Men from Indian Myths & Legends

By Shahrukh Husain • Illustrated by Durga Prasad Das

Summary

This is part of the World Mythology Series, and it begins with "The World of the Ancient Indians" and explains that the universe of Hindu myths consists of three worlds: physical, heavenly, and spiritual. Sections follow on "The Old Gods" and "The Great Goddesses." Mentioned here are Indra (rain and dew), Surya (the sun), Agni (fire), Shakti (the Universal Mother), Savitri (wisdom and learning), and Lakshmi or Shri (good fortune).

In "The Holy Men of India," the reader learns of seven holy men, or *rishis*, created by Brahma. A section is devoted to "Shiv, God of Destruction," who can change his appearance and is lord of goblins, demons, and wandering spirits.

"The Many Forms of Vishnu" explores the Hindu god who is most widely worshiped, while "The Adventures of Ram" tells of a robber who is transformed into a person of enormous spiritual power. "The Life of Krishna" examines the god Vishnu in human form explaining humanity's role in the pattern of the universe.

There are "Stories from the Mahabbarat" coming from a long epic, "Legends of Romance and Adventure; Stories of Wit and Trickery," and a final section, "Tales of Kings and Princes."

Shocken, 1987. 132 pp. Color and black & white illustrations. ISBN 0-8052-4028-4

Activities

With Librarian Guidance

Encourage students to explore atlases that are available in the library. A new edition of *The Times Atlas of the World* (Times Books) would be an excellent reference. Then ask a small group of interested students to make a large map showing how the world of the ancient Indians has been divided into modern day countries. It should include Afghanistan, Bangladesh, Bhutan, India, Nepal, Pakistan, and Sri Lanka and should show the Himalayas, the Arabian Sea and the Bay of Bengal. The students' completed map should be posted on a bulletin board.

With Classroom Teacher Guidance

1. Hinduism became the principal religion of South Asia. Ask a pair of students to research this topic and write a paper which includes a bibliography to share with the class. When did Hinduism begin? What are its main tenets? Ask the students to share the highlights of their report orally, and post the completed paper on a bulletin board or on a school Web site.

2. "Damayanti's Choice" could be re-written and made into a simple and attractive picture book. Invite a small group of students to collaborate and prepare the text for a 32-page picture book. The story could be divided into scenes and printed with a word processing program. The same students, or others, could volunteer to illustrate the book. Then one of the students should arrange to visit a primary-grade classroom and read and present the book to the class.

The Dwarf, the Giant, and the Unicorn
A Tale of King Arthur
Retold by James Cross Giblin • Illustrated by Claire Ewart

Summary

This story is a retelling of an Arthurian romance written in the late fifteenth or early sixteenth century. As the story begins, young Arthur becomes king and sets out with his knights on his first sea voyage. Caught in a terrible storm, they land on the beach of an island. The boat is stuck fast, so King Arthur sets out on his horse to see if there are others on the island who can help. He comes upon a strange tower. When he calls up to the window of the tower, he is greeted by a dwarf who asks that Arthur stay and hear his story.

The dwarf tells King Arthur that he and his pregnant wife were left on the island. Shortly after delivering a baby, his wife died, and the dwarf sought shelter beneath a tree with his baby. Three baby unicorns were there, and the mother unicorn returned and found them. The mother nursed the baby and killed a deer for the dwarf to eat. The son grew into a giant.

When the dwarf's son returns, King Arthur and the dwarf convince him that Arthur is friendly and could even take them back to their own country if the giant helped. The next morning, King Arthur, the dwarf, the giant, and the unicorn return to the ship. The giant frees it from the beach, and they all sail safely back to Camelot.

Clarion, 1996. 48 pp. Full-color illustrations. ISBN 0-395-60520-2

Activities

With Librarian Guidance

1. Reading this book may pique interest in reading more books involving the Arthurian legends. Gather some of these books: **The Sword in the Stone,** by T.H. White (Philomel, 1993, 256p.); **The Kitchen Knight: A Tale of King Arthur,** by Margaret Hodges (Holiday House, 1990, 30pp.); **The Legend of King Arthur,** by Robin Lister, (Doubleday, 1989, 93pp.) and make them available. After students read one of these books, ask them to write a book review. Post the reviews on a bulletin board or on a school Web site.

2. The author won two Golden Kite Awards. The librarian may have a vertical file devoted to children's book awards, or may keep back issues of journals that report awards. Using available resources, have two students research the Golden Kite Award and write a short report for the class sharing what they learn. How long has the award existed? When is the award given? Who determines the winner? What book was the most recent winner? What is the award given for?

With Parent/Caregiver Guidance

The librarian or classroom teacher might send home the following letter.

Dear Parent: Your child has just read The Dwarf, the Giant, and the Unicorn: A Tale of King Arthur *(summary attached). In the story, the mother unicorn cannot speak, yet she appears able to communicate with the dwarf and the giant. Your child may want to discuss with you ways in which real animals communicate with humans. Your child should take notes on your conversation and be able to participate in a class discussion on this topic.*

Fabled Cities, Princes & Jinn From Arab Myths and Legends

By Khairat Al-Saleh • Illustrated by Rashad Salim

Summary

This book is one of the World Mythology Series and contains 40 stories. The first portion, "The Arabs and Their World,"describes the fertile lands of ancient Arabia. The second section, "Gods of the Ancient Arabs," deals with Mecca in Saudi Arabia, where the Prophet Muhammad was born. The author describes the worship of idols, explains about sacred animals, trees, wells, and rocks, and discusses the major gods.

In "Myths and Legends of the Extinct Arabs," the stories of legendary people are told. Surviving Arabs are divided into two groups: Arabs of the North and Arabs of the South. Their stories are included in the section "Myths and Legends of the North and South." They include stories of kings and queens.

These early Arabs believed that priests had contact with the supernatural and had familiar spirits that were jinns or demons. Priests also assumed roles of wise men and judges. The section on "Priests, Soothsayers and Wise Men" tells their stories.

The final sections deal with "Tales of Generosity, Honour and Loyalty, Celestial and Terrestrial Worlds, Angels and Jinn, The Arabian Nights, The City of Brass," and "Journeys to the World of the Supernatural."

Peter Bedrick, 1985. 132 pp. Full-color illustrations and line art. ISBN 0-87226-924-8

Activities

With Librarian Guidance

Students may wish to learn more about the Prophet Muhammad. In addition to research in print materials, students might visit **http://www.usc.edu/dept/MSA/fundamentals/prophet**. This page allows students to read a biography of Muhammad written by a Muslim and/or by a non-Muslim. They can see examples of Muhammad's teachings, learn what he was like, read his last sermon, and find out what other scholars say about him. Using notes, have these students share their findings with the class.

With Classroom Teacher Guidance

Because camels were so essential to Arabs, they were highly revered. Ask two students to write a research paper on camels. What types are there? Where do they live? What interesting characteristics do they have? Ask the students to write a paper with a bibliography listing at least three sources of information. They should also visit **http://www.phillyzoo.org/pz0068.htm**. Here they will have the opportunity via e-mail to ask any camel-related questions of a docent at the zoo.

With Parent/Caregiver Guidance

The classroom teacher or librarian might duplicate this letter to parents.

Dear Parent: Your child has read some Arabian myths and legends (summary attached). One of the proverbs mentioned in the reading is: "He who does good has good done unto him." Your child may want to discuss this with you. He or she is to write an original short story where this proverb will be an appropriate last line.

Favorite Norse Myths

Retold by Mary Pope Osborne • Illustrated by Troy Howell

Summary

The author explains in the introduction that before the year 1000, old Norse stories were told about the creation of the earth and battles between gods and giants. Two collections of these old stories were gathered, *The Poetic Edda* and *The Prose Edda*. They are the primary sources for the pre-Christian stories of old Norway. These Norse myths have many features in common with the myths of other lands.

This book contains fourteen myths: "Creation: The Nine Worlds, Odin's Three Quests, The Magic Stallion, How Thor Got His Hammer, Loki's Children, The Giant's Bride, The Golden Apples, The Fairest Feet, Spell of the Giant King, Marriage of the Ice Maiden, The Giant's Cauldron, Thor and the Clay Giant, The Death of Balder," and "Twilight of the Gods."

Much of the art work in this book was inspired by the simple images left behind by the Vikings. These were often carved in stone, bone and wood. Each chapter contains a primitive style drawing based on Viking art and then a full-color dramatic painting with the primitive version scratched on its surface.

The book contains a bibliography, an index, and lengthy notes giving additional information about Norse Myths.

Scholastic, 1996. 88 pp. Full-color illustrations. ISBN 0-590-48046-4

Activities

With Librarian Guidance

During the Age of the Vikings from 780 to 1070, Vikings attacked villages in Britain, France, Germany and Spain. The Vikings from Norway also sailed to Greenland and North America. Invite students to do further research on the Vikings and to make a map showing their travels. Post the completed map of Viking travels on a library or classroom bulletin board. The following books will be useful: ***The Vikings,*** by Kathryn Hinds (Marshall Cavendish, 1998, 80pp.); ***Explorers & Traders***, by Claire Craig (Time-Life Books, 1996, 64pp.); and ***Viking Explorers***, by Luigi Pruneti (P. Bedrick Books, 1995, 48pp.).

With Classroom Teacher Guidance

In the story "Creation: The Nine Worlds," the reader learns that Odin and his brothers caught sparks from the fires of Muspell and turned them into stars. Have students compare this story with Native American star myths such as those found in *They Dance in the Sky.* In a book discussion group, have students discuss how these stories are alike and how they are different.

With Parent/Caregiver Guidance

Ask for parent volunteers to work with a small drama group. The group will rehearse and act out "The Giant's Bride" for the rest of the class. Have the parent volunteers and students re-read the story, select parts (Loki, Freya, Thor, Odin, Thrym, and miscellaneous giants), and make very simple costumes using sheets and a veil. A necessary prop will be Thor's hammer.

The Golden Hoard
Myths and Legends of the World
By Geraldine McCaughrean • Illustrated by Bee Willey

Summary

This collection contains twenty-two myths and legends, some familiar and some new to most readers. Included are: "The Golden Wish" (Greek myth), "Shooting the Sun" (Chinese myth), "George and the Dragon" (Persian myth), "Skinning Out" (Ethiopian myth), "Robin Hood and the Golden Arrow" (English legend), "Brave Quest" (Native American myth), "Saving Time" (Polynesian myth), "The Lake That Flew Away" (an Estonian legend), "Admirable Hare," (legend from Ceylon), "All Roads Lead to Wales" (Welsh legend), "Rainbow Snake" (Australian myth), "Juno's Roman Geese" (Roman legend), "John Barleycorn" (American myth), "The Singer Above the River" (German legend), "How Music Was Fetched Out of Heaven" (Mexican myth), "Whose Footprints?" (myth from the Gold Coast), "The Death of El Cid," (Spanish legend), "The Man Who Almost Lived Forever" (Mesopotamian legend), "Stealing Heaven's Thunder" (Norse myth), "Anansi and the Mind of God" (West Indian myth), "How Men and Women Finally Agreed" (Kikuyu myth), and "First Snow" (Native American myth).

There are brief notes about each of the stories at the end of the book.

M. K. McElderry, 1995. 130 pp. Full-color illustrations. ISBN 0-689-80741-4

Activities

With Librarian Guidance

The Spanish legend tells of "The Death of El Cid." Have a group of students research El Cid (Don Rodrigo Diaz de Vivar). Among sources of information, consider *El Cid,* by Geraldine McCaughrean (Oxford Illustrated Classics, 1989, 128pp.), and *El Cid,* by Philip Koslow (Chelsea House, 1993, 111pp.). Students might visit **http://www.camelotintl.com/heritage/cid.htm** and other sites on the Web. What facts are known about the legendary figure? Ask these students to make an oral report to the class sharing what they learn.

With Classroom Teacher Guidance

"Juno's Roman Geese" tells of a statue that almost seems to come alive. Most towns have statues to extol pioneers, soldiers, inventors, etc. Ask a group of students to make a statue map of your town or city. The Chamber of Commerce might supply students with a city map and helpful information. On the map, indicate with symbols where various statues are located. Post the map on a classroom bulletin board or on a school Web site.

With Parent/Caregiver Guidance

In "All Roads Lead to Wales," the princes play chess. Some members of the class will no doubt be chess players. Ask a parent who plays chess to organize a chess class that will meet once a week after school for a month. The parent, or a guest invited by the parent, could teach some chess strategy at each of the four sessions, and then allow time for participants to play.

How the Animals Got Their Colors
Animal Myths from Around the World
By Michael Rosen • Illustrated by John Clementson

Summary

The first story in the book, "Coyote," is a Zuni tale which explains how coyotes got such angry-looking yellow eyes. The "Flying Fish" is a story commonly told on the northeast coast of Papua, which is a province located on the Pacific island of New Guinea.

"Frog" is an ancient Greek story that was retold by the Roman poet Ovid in his book *Metamorphoses.* "Tiger" is a tale that comes from the far north mountain region of China. "Brolga" is a myth told by the aborigines of Northern Australia. "Leopard" is a story that comes from the Loma tribe of the central mountains of Liberia. It explains about tribal law and customs.

"Peacock" is a myth told by the Khasi people who live in the East Khasi Hills of India. The peacock is often shown in these myths to be vain and fond of luxury. "Crane" is a myth that comes from Uganda, in the Lake region of East Africa. The final story in the book, "How the Animals Got Their Colors," is a creation myth of the Ayoreo Indians. These Indians came from a part of South American that is now known as Bolivia and Paraguay.

Short notes about the stories and about the featured animals are given in the back of the book.

Harcourt Brace Jovanovich, 1992. 48 pp. Full-color illustrations. ISBN 0-15-236783-7

Activities

With Librarian Guidance

Although coyotes are numerous, their close canine relatives, the wolves, are endangered in 47 of the 48 lower United States. Have a group of students research endangered wolves. They can visit **http://www.afternet.com/ ~ teal/species-else.html** on the Web and by clicking on "photos of North American endangered species" see pictures of endangered animals. A click on "What is a wolf?" will give more information. Another helpful tool would be **Encyclopedia of Endangered Species** (Gale Research, 1994). Additional useful resources are **The Wolf,** by Michael S. Dahl (Capstone Press, 1997, 48pp.) and **Journey of the Red Wolf,** by Roland Smith (Dutton, 1996, 59pp.).

With Classroom Teacher Guidance

The story "Frog" is presented as a riddle. Once students have read this story, they may use it as a model to write their own animal riddles. They might work alone or in pairs. Allow time for students to share the riddles they write and for their classmates to try to guess the answers.

With Parent/Caregiver Guidance

Invite a parent to work with four students in a drama group. The parent will read and direct the students in a presentation of the "Tiger" story which is a contest between tiger, thunder, echo, and dragon. The students will need a few simple costumes and props as they adapt this story into a play. When ready, they can perform their play for the class.

Hungry Woman
The Myths and Legends of the Aztecs
Edited by John Bierhorst

Summary

The first section of the book contains Creation Myths: "The Hungry Woman; The First Sun; Monkeys, Turkeys, and Fish; Up from the Dead Land; True Corn; The Fifth Sun; The Origin of Music;" and "Quetzalcoatl in Tula."

The second section, "The Fall of Tula," describe a pre-Aztec empire: "The King's Daughter and the Pepper Man, The Sorcerer's Dance, Master Log," and "The Flight of Quetzalcoatl."

Stories of the rise and fall of Mexico and the coming of Christianity make up the third section, "The Founding of Mexico." Included are: "The Birth of Huitzilopochtli, Copil's Heart, The Woman of Discord," and "The Eagle on the Prickly Pear."

The fourth section, "In the Days of Montezuma," includes: "The Talking Stone, Montezuma's Wound, Eight Omens, The Return of Quetzalcoatl," and "Is It You?"

The final section, "After Cortez," is the longest and contains: "How the World Began; Calling the Ghost of Montezuma; The Virgin of Guadalupe; The Weeping Woman: The Prince and the Seamstress; The Weeping Woman: Cortez and the Malintzin;" and "The Weeping Woman: Forever Without Rest."

William Morrow 1984. 148 pp. Reproductions of black-and-white miniature paintings done by Aztec artists of the sixteenth century. ISBN 0-688-02766-0

Activities

With Librarian Guidance

1. To gain more background knowledge about the Aztecs, have a pair of students gather information from **http://www.wsu.edu:8000/ ~ dee/CIVAMRCA/AZTECS.htm.** They should take notes from the wealth of information at this Web site and be ready to share orally with the class what they learn about Aztec history, the Tenochtitlan Ruins, the economy and society, religion, human sacrifice and the Wall of Skulls, the Great Temple Stairs, and Aztec writing.

2. The last of Mexico's kings to rule as emperor was Montezuma, who died in June of 1520. Ask a pair of students to research Montezuma. Besides an encyclopedia, useful resources include: ***The Sad Night: The Story of an Aztec Victory and a Spanish Loss*** (Clarion, 1994, 40pp.) and ***Montezuma's Missing Treasure,*** by Anita Larsen (Crestwood House, 1992, 48pp.).

With Classroom Teacher Guidance:

Some students love the challenge of a mystery. One of the creation myths discusses the "Jaguar Sun," a constellation that dips into the ocean each night. Invite a pair of students to try to find out which constellation of stars might be the Jaguar Sun. Who in the community might be a good resource? Is there an observatory near by? Is there a college or university with an astronomy department? Students should bring in a drawing of the constellation to put on a classroom bulletin board and describe how they tracked down the needed information.

Land of the Long White Cloud
Maori Myths, Tales and Legends
By Kiri Te Kanawa • Illustrated by Michael Foreman

Summary

When Polynesian sailors discovered New Zealand, land of the Long White Cloud, they brought with them myths, poems, and chants. The stories in this book explain why and how so many of the places in New Zealand have special names.

The following stories are included: "The Birth of Maui; Maui and the Great Fish; Maui Tames the Sun; Kupe's Discovery of Aotearoa; Hinemoa and Tutanekai; Kahukura and the Fairies; The Talking Taniwha of Rotorua; Te Kanawa and the Visitors by Firelight; Mataora and the Niwareka in the Underworld; Legends about Lakes, Rivers and Trees; The Enchanted Hunting-Ground; The Trees of the Forest; Lake Te Anau; Hotu-puku; Patawai; Rona and the Legend of the Moon; Hutu and Pare; Three Little Bird Legends; The Ground Parrot and the Albatross; Kakariki and Kata;" and "Maui and the Birds."

Many of these stories are about mischievous Maui, a god who fishes around South Island and who was raised by Tama, a powerful sea god. Other stories are creation myths, legends of various Maori tribes that include monsters and trips into the underground spirit world, as well as tales of romance and adventure.

Arcade, 1989. 119 pp. Full-color illustrations. ISBN 1-86205-075-9

Activities

With Librarian Guidance

Kahukura brings a net to his village to show his people how to catch fish. Nets have proved to be problematic when tuna fishermen catch dolphin in their nets. Invite two students to research this topic and then orally report back to the class what they learn. Students may want to check the **Index to The New York Times** for available articles on microfilm. Another source would be the index to *Facts on File.* For magazine articles on dolphin, students could search the *Reader's Guide to Periodical Literature* as well as the *Subject Index to Children's Magazines.*

With Classroom Teacher Guidance

Ask two students to make and post a large map of the North and South Islands of New Zealand. (They might use an opaque projector to produce a large image of an available blank map.) The students should use colors to indicate elevation so that mountains and valleys are clearly visible. As events happen in the tales included in this book, students should put names of places in appropriate spots on the map. Include Cook Strait, Tara, Wellington, Lake Rotorua, the small islands that Kupe carved off of North Island and South Island, etc.

With Guidance from Music Teacher

Ask the music educator in your school to locate some recordings of Dame Kiri Te Kanawa, who is both the author of this book as well as a famous opera singer. Play some of these recordings for the class.

The Long-Haired Girl

By Doreen Rappaport • Illustrated by Yang Ming-Yi

Summary

As the story opens, there is a drought. The villagers from the Lei-gong Mountains, including a young girl named Ah-mei, must walk to a stream two miles away to fetch buckets of water.

One day Ah-mei climbs the mountain behind her house looking for herbs. She pulls out a long, white turnip. As water trickles out of the hole where the turnip had been growing, the turnip jumps out of her hand and re-seals the hole.

The god of thunder, Lei-gong, appears and threatens to kill Ah-mei if she tells anyone about the secret spring. And for a month, she tells no one, but during this time she becomes pale and her hair turns white. One day, when Ah-mei sees how desperate an old man becomes after spilling water, she leads the villagers to the spring where they chisel at the hole until water gushes down the mountain.

Lei-gong says Ah-mei must die and lie on the cliff beneath the water. Ah-mei goes to bid farewell to her mother. The old man she helped now says he will save her. He has a stone figure of Ah-mei. As Ah-mei's hair touches the statue's head, it takes root. The statue is put on the cliff and fools Lei-gong. Ah-mei's hair grows in black again, and she and the villagers no longer fear drought because they have White Hair Falls.

Dial, 1995. 32 pp. Colored woodcut illustrations. ISBN 0-8037-1411-4

Activities

With Librarian Guidance

The last picture in the book shows rice paddies. Invite a pair of students to find out how rice is cultivated in China. Some useful reference books are **China**, by Pat Ryan (Child's World, 1998, 32pp.) and **China**, by Ann Heinricks (Children's Press, 1997, 47pp.). Students might visit the Web site **http://cityguide-uk.lycos.com/asia/china/CHNGuiyang.html.** Guiyang is the capital of China's south-central province, Guizhan, which has a subtropical climate good for growing rice. Students should orally share with the class what they learn.

With Classroom Teacher Guidance

1. Ah-mei is pictured in front of a banyan tree. Ask two students to research this topic and report to the class what they learn. They might want to read **In the Heart of the Village: The World of the Indian Banyan Tree**, by Barbara Bash (Sierra Club Books for Children, 1996.) What does a banyan tree look like? Where do these trees grow in the world? How big are they? Can they find a picture to share of a banyan tree? Additional information can be found on the banyan tree home page, **http://192.216.191.149/RainForest/Vines/4287/.**

2. The pictures in this book were made from wood-cuts. Invite a knowledgeable local artist to visit the class, bringing in examples and explaining how wood-cuts are made and used. Follow up the visit with a thank you note written by one or more of the students.

Moontellers
Myths of the Moon from Around the World
By Lynn Moroney • Illustrated by Greg Shed

Summary

The viewpoints and attitudes toward the moon of eleven cultures are revealed in the short stories contained in this book. The first story, "Moon Man," is from Euahlayi, Australia and tells how an embarrassed moon grows round and then shrinks away. The story, "Rabbit and Frog," from China describes what happens to Lady Heng-O and her potion.

The Iroquois legend of "Weaver and Cat" tells how a cat unravels an old woman's weaving causing her to begin anew each month. "Moon Woman," is a Polynesian story which explains how Hina makes the clouds that cover the earth. The Aztec story from Mexico, "Rabbit," tells of a time when there were two suns and it was too bright. From Yuracare, Bolivia, comes "Four-Eyed Jaguar," and how he was saved from a hunter by hurling himself to the moon.

The Louchieux of Canada see a "Bare-Legged Boy," when they study the moon, while the Scandinavians describe "Boy and Girl with a Pail." Musicians in India see "Handprints" when they look at the moon. In "Brush Burner," American cowboys tell of someone burning brush on the moon. From Africa comes the story of "Drummer," who lives on the moon. "Moon Seas" gives a scientific version by an astronomer on the face of the moon. The book concludes with suggestions for further reading.

Northland, 1995. 32 pp. Full-color illustrations. ISBN 0-87358-601-8

Activities

With Librarian Guidance

Have a small group of students carry out research on clocks and calendars. At **http://www.physics.nist.gov/GenInt/Time/ancient.html** students can click on an ancient calendar, early clocks, revolution in time keeping, the atomic age, world time scales, and NIST time calibration. A number of nonfiction books will also be useful to the group including *Exploring Time,* by Gillian Chapman and Pam Robson (Millbrook Press, 1995) and *Sun-Day, Moon-Day: How the Week Was Made* (Barefoot Books, 1998).

With Classroom Teacher Guidance

Invite a pair of students to create a phases-of-the-moon calendar. These students should cut out shapes that will represent the various phases of the moon (new moon, quarter moon, half moon, three-quarter moon, full moon.) Each night the students should check the moon, discuss together the next morning what they observed, and then glue the correct phase of the moon shape onto a calendar hung on a class bulletin board.

With Parent/Caregiver Guidance

The librarian or classroom teacher might duplicate the following letter and send it home:

Dear Parent: Your child has read Moontellers: Myths of the Moon from Around the World *(summary attached). During the next few nights, would you and your child spend a few minutes studying the moon and using your imagination? Can you imagine pictures on the moon's surface? Your child should make a sketch of what you see and be prepared to describe this in class.*

Myths and Legends from Around the World

by Sandy Shepherd • Illustrated by Tudor Humphries

Summary

This book contains more than 50 short stories which are arranged thematically: "The World We Live In, The Heavens and the Earth, Founders and Inventors, Heroes and Heroines, Gods and Spirits," and "Good and Evil." The myths and legends in this book come from all over the world, so a world map is included to help the readers identify countries where the different legends originated.

In each chapter, there is a myth about daily life. These stories provide insight into the ways people in the past lived in different parts of the world. Other sections try to explain why the world is the way it is and why people behave as they do. Some of these stories involve gods, goddesses, and spirits.

Included are creation stories from Japan, Tahiti, Egypt, Scandinavia, North America, Guatemala, New Zealand, and India. There are stories explaining about plants and animals from Sierra Leone, Canada, Greece, and Russia. Stories about gods and goddesses include the earth goddess, the divine archer, the sun, moon, and stars. There is also the flood story of Matsya and stories about the forces of nature including volcanoes. Discoverers, inventors, and founders of cities have become part of myths, as have the great deities and the forces of good and evil.

Evans Brothers, 1994. 96 pp. Full-color illustrations. ISBN 0-237-51488-5

Activities

With Librarian Guidance

The cat is one of the animal gods from Egypt. Some cats were embalmed and turned into mummies. Invite a pair of students to do some research. Has a cat mummy ever been found? Where? Ask the students to report what they learn to the class through an oral report. They might visit the Preserved for Posterity site (**http://www.lam.mus.ca.us/cats/C33/index.htm**) which is maintained by the Natural History Museum of Los Angeles County. They will find information and pictures of a cat mummy and sarcophagus. More information can be found at **http://members.home.net/msteele/cathist.htm**.

With Classroom Teacher Guidance

We continue to read in our newspapers and magazines about new inventions and discoveries. Ask students to choose a topic mentioned in the section on Founders and Inventors and write about it not as a myth or legend, but as a newspaper account. Post the completed newspaper stories on a bulletin board or on a school Web site.

With Parent/Caregiver Guidance

Many science project books contain simple directions for making a sun dial. One good resource is **Science for Kids: 39 Easy Astronomy Experiments** by Robert W. Wood (TAB Books, 1991). Duplicate these directions (with permission) and send them home with a note.

Dear Parent: Your child is bringing home directions on how to make a simple sun dial. Your help in assisting the student to complete this project and return it to school will be appreciated.

Of Swords and Sorcerers
The Adventures of King Arthur and His Knights
By Margaret Hodges and Margery Gvernden • Illustrated by David Frampton

---

Summary

The book is divided into nine chapters, each dealing with a phase in the life of King Arthur. "Of Castles and Dragons" tells how King Vortigern discovered Merlin the Magician as a boy, how Uther Pendragon took Vortigern's place, and how Uther and Igraine let Merlin hide their young son, Arthur.

"Of Swords and Sorcerers" describes Arthur as a young king who receives his sword from the Lady of the Lake and wards off the attempts of his half-sister, Morgan le Fay, to remove him as king. "Of Guinevere and the Round Table" tells how Arthur fights to save Camelot and win the hand of Guinevere, whose father gives him the Round Table as a wedding gift.

"Of True Love" tells how Lancelot claims a seat at the Round Table. In "Of the Sword Bridge," Queen Guinevere is captured by Sir Malagant and Lancelot rescues her. "Of the Boy Who Would Be a Knight" describes how Percival joins the Round Table, and "Of the Coming of Sir Galahad," explains how the Seat of Danger at the Round Table is filled. "Of the Quest for the Holy Grail" tells of Galahad's search. "Of the Last Battle" tells how Arthur is wounded by Sir Mordred, how Guinevere goes to a nunnery, and how Lancelot lives his final years as a monk.

Charles Scribner's, 1993. 96 pp. Illustrated with black-and-white woodcuts. ISBN 0-684-19437-6

Activities

With Librarian Guidance

King Arthur's father was from Cornwall, and Percival came from Wales. Have students research Cornwall and Wales using four kinds of resources (encyclopedia, magazine, reference book, Web site.) Possible resources include: ***Compton's Interactive Encyclopedia, European Travel & Life Magazine, Great Britain,*** by Anna Sproule (Silver Burdett, 1991), and **http://city.net/countries/united_kingdom/england/cornwall.**

With Classroom Teacher Guidance

Since students are consumers and users, they are good judges of the quality of the many current computer games which feature sorcerers and/or knights in armor. Invite students who have played these games to write a review of them. What is the game's name? Who makes it? Where is it available? What are its main features? What good and bad points does it have? Would you recommend it? Post these reviews on a bulletin board or school Web site.

With Parent/Caregiver Guidance

The librarian or classroom teacher might duplicate and send home the following note:

Dear Parent: Your child has read Of Swords and Sorcerers *(summary attached). Knights often had beautiful designs on their shields. Either by doing research and showing historical designs, or using imagination and creating original shield designs, students are to make a shield at home from cardboard, decorate it, and bring it to school to display on a bulletin board. Please discuss with your child what symbols might be used and their meaning.*

Ordinary Splendors
Tales of Virtues and Wisdom
By Toni Knapp • Illustrated by Kevin Sohl

Summary

The colorful artwork in this book was done by a boy between his eighth and fourteenth birthdays. Proceeds of this book will help the Scott Newman Center to develop innovative drug education and prevention technologies for children and families.

This book is divided into three sections: "Water," "Land," and "Sky." The four stories in the "Water" section include: "Arion and the Dolphin" (ancient Greece), "The Young Crab and Her Mother" (an Aesop fable), "The Rainbow Fish" (Russian folktale), and "The Little Blond Shark" (parable from Hawaii).

The "Land" section includes: "The Giraffe's Long Neck" (adapted from an ancient Bushman legend), "The Prince and the Rhinoceros" (India), "The Elephant Puzzle" (legend from India), "The Tortoise and the Hare" (an Aesop fable), "King Bruce and the Spider" (legend from Scotland), "The Grasshopper, the Mouse, the Bee, and the Harp" (fairytale from Ireland), "The Hedgehog" (British folklore), and "Rat and the Chinese Zodiac" (China).

The final section of the book, "Sky," includes "The Eagle and the Shrike" (Cherokee legend), "Mariposa the Butterfly" (traditional Mexican tale), "The Buzzard and the Dove" (Mayans of Guatemala), "Two Birds" (adapted from an Eastern European fable), and "Owl" (anonymous four-line poem).

Roberts Rinehart, 1995. 46 pp. Full-color illustrations. ISBN 1-57098-003-9

Activities

With Librarian Guidance

"Arion and the Dolphin" describes human/dolphin interaction. There have been many recent magazine stories that describe attempts to communicate and train dolphin and dangers of dolphin being caught in fishing nets. Ask a small group of students to use UnCover or the *Guide to Periodical Literature* to locate magazine articles about dolphins and to make a detailed list of these. Try to secure copies of these articles and have them available in a vertical file for further student research.

With Classroom Teacher Guidance

Many schools have programs which deal with substance abuse prevention and which impart accurate information about drugs. If there is such a program in your school, two students might want to write to the Scott Newman Center (6255 Sunset Boulevard, Suite 1906, Los Angeles, CA 90028-7420) requesting free information. They should include a 9 x 12-inch, self-addressed stamped envelope and share with the class any information they receive.

With Parent/Caregiver Guidance

The librarian or classroom teacher might duplicate and send home the following note:

Dear Parent: Each student is being asked to contribute to a bulletin board on the names of various groups of animals. For example, a group of dolphin is called a pod. A group of fish is a school. Each student is being asked to discuss this at home, complete the blank below, and bring it to school with a magazine picture or photocopy to illustrate it.

A group of _____ is called a _____.

Realms of Gold, Myths & Legends from Around the World

By Ann Pilling • Illustrated by Kady MacDonald Denton

Summary

This anthology is in three parts. In the first part, there are myths in which people attempt to explain the wonders that they see in the world around them. They seek to answer questions such as: Why are there stars in the sky? and Why is there fire? The second part contains stories that explore the themes of love and death. In these stories, there is beauty, heartbreak, and sacrifice. And the final section explores tales of fools and heroes. These may be stories of great foolishness or of great and noble adventure. The stories included come from many different countries.

The section called "Earth, Air, Fire, and Water" contains "Iyadola's Babies" (West African), "Naming the Winds" (Iroquois), "How Maui Stole Fire From the Gods" (Pacific), "Water, Moon and Sun" (Nigerian).

The section on "Love and Death" contains: "The Death of Balder" (Norse), "Persephone" (Greek), "Bedd Gelert" (Welsh), "The Hare in the Moon" (Indian), "The Unicorn" (Celtic), and "The Willow Pattern Story" (Chinese).

The final section, "Fools and Heroes" includes: "King Midas" (Greek), "The Wishing Fish" (Russian), "The Giants Who Couldn't Swim" (Irish), and "How Perseus Killed the Gorgon" (Greek).

Kingfisher, 1993. 93 pp. Color illustrations. ISBN 1-85697-913-X

Activities

With Librarian Guidance

In "The Unicorn," Rhiannon gathers truffles. Ask two students to research truffles. What are they? Where are they found? Are animals used to help locate them? Ask the students to write a short paper on the topic including a bibliography listing at least three sources of information. These resources might prove helpful: **http://www.herb.lsa.umich.edu/kidpage/truffind.htm**, *Discovering Fungi*, by Jennifer Coldrey (Bookwright Press, 1988), ***Katya's Book of Mushrooms,*** by Arnold Katya (Holt, 1997).

With Classroom Teacher Guidance

On page 57, there is a picture of a plate which shows "The Willow Pattern Story." It is very likely that someone in your school community will own some pieces of this willow pattern. Perhaps you could advertise for an owner in your school newsletter. If someone is identified, ask the guest to bring a plate to class, and with the students identify the scenes on the plate that tell the story. Be sure to follow up with a thank you letter to the guest.

With Parent/Caregiver Guidance

Invite a parent volunteer to work with a small puppetry group. "Water, Moon, and Sun" could be presented as a puppet show. Stick puppets could be made to represent Sun, Moon, whales, fish, and crabs. A piece of blue cloth, thrown across the stage could be water. After the students make their puppets and practice the show, they could present it to a class in the school.

Russian Tales and Legends

Retold by Charles Downing • Illustrated by Joan Kiddell-Monroe

Summary

This classic collection of Russian stories has been reprinted many times and is part of the Oxford Myths and Legends Series paperback editions.

The book is divided into two sections. The first section (Byliny) contains Heroic Poems: "Volga; Svyatogor's Bride; Dunay; Dobrynia and Alyosha; Ilya of Murom and Svyatogor; Ilya of Murom and Nightingale the Robber; The Three Journeys of Ilya of Murom; Stavr Godinovich and his Clever Wife; Sadko the Minstrel; Vasili Buslayevich; Vasili Buslayevich's Pilgrimage;" and "Since When There Have Been No More Heroes in Holy Russia."

The second section of the book (Skazki) contains Folk-Tales, including: "Death and the Soldier; I-Know-Not-What of I-Know-Not Where; Sorrow; The Mountain of Gold; The Russian and the Tartar; The Soldier Who Did Not Wash; The Crock of Gold; One-Eyed Likho; The Death Watch; The Fool and the Birch-Tree; Fair Vasilissa and Baba Yaga; The Frost, the Sun, and the Wind; The Angel; The Magic Berries; The Firebird; The Hired Man; The Fortunate Maiden;" and "The Wife Who Liked Fairy-tales."

The book also contains a short glossary.

Oxford University, 1996. 214 pp. Black and white illustrations. ISBN 0-19-274144-6

Activities

With Librarian Guidance

The story "Dunay" tells how the River Danube sprang forth from the spot where Dunay fell to the ground. Ask two students to research the Danube River and share with the class what they learn. How long is it? Of what importance is the Danube? What environmental problems are there? Their report should include a map on which the students have traced the river's route. Students need access to a good atlas such as *The Times Atlas of the World, Britannica Atlas,* or *McGraw Hill Illustrated World Geography.* Useful books include *Great Rivers,* a six-volume set (Marshall Cavendish, 1997), and *Rivers,* by Terry Jennings (Silver Burdett, 1998). The Web site **http://www.rivernet.org/danube.htm** will provide information on the Danube and several environmental projects.

With Classroom Teacher Guidance

Ask students to complete one of the two following writing assignments, posting the completed stories on a bulletin board or on a school Web site.

◆ Many stories of competitions between the elements, such as "The Frost, the Sun, and the Wind" have been written. Interested students should write their own stories in which a competition is held. They may use other weather-related phenomenon such as clouds, rain, rainbows, snow, etc.

◆ On page 102, Masha says, "morning is wiser than evening." Ask students to write an original story in which someone is struggling with a problem. Instead of acting hastily, the person waits until morning and then is able to solve the problem.

William Tell

Written and illustrated by Leonard Everett Fisher

Summary

The story begins in 1307 when the Swiss were oppressed by the Hapsburg rulers. A proclamation states that the royal governor's hat will be mounted on a pole in Gessler Square. Failure to kneel to this hat will result in severe punishment.

Among the people in the square is a famous hunter, William Tell, who is passing by with his son, Jemmy. The people are afraid of the tyrant, Hermann Gessler, and begin kneeling to the hat. When a young man with a pig rushes by without kneeling, he is arrested. A young boy races by, chased by his sister. Since they do not stop to kneel, they are both are arrested.

Then William Tell and his son walk by the hat, deliberately not kneeling. The royal governor threatens to lock them up, but then he comes up with a different plan. William Tell is to shoot one arrow at an apple placed on his son's head. If he fails, William Tell will be locked up for life. If he succeeds, Tell's life will be spared and no one need kneel before the hat again.

Tell accepts the challenge but takes a second arrow with him. He splits the apple on his son's head, but then admits that the second arrow was for Hermann Gessler if he had missed. Tell is locked in prison, but escapes a week later and kills Gessler, freeing the people and becoming a hero.

Farrar, Straus & Giroux, 1996. 32 pp. Full-color illustrations. ISBN 0 374-38436-3

Activities

With Librarian Guidance

Many other books have been written about William Tell. Invite two students to use the library's computerized or card catalog to locate other books about this legendary figure. Have the students make a list of other books including title, author, publisher, and publication date. Use the list to borrow books through interlibrary loan so that students can do further reading. On the Web at **http://www.users.dircon.co.uk/~nonsuch/dict/glossary/willtell.htm** students will also find a brief version of the story.

With Classroom Teacher Guidance

After students have read the book, hold a class discussion. Ask students whether or not Hermann Gessler's law that required everyone to bow to his hat was a just or an unjust law. What was the purpose of the law? Do students think that the people who obeyed the law were cowards or wise men? Ask students to explain why they feel as they do.

With Parent/Caregiver Guidance

The teacher might send home the following note:

Dear Parent: Your child has read William Tell *(summary attached). As a follow-up activity, we are making original hats from simple materials and will wear them during a special "hat day." If you could assist on (provide date and time) please sign this slip and return it. (Clare Beton's book,* Hats: Lots of Simple Step-By-Step Ideas, *[Warwick Press, 1990], or a similar arts and crafts book would be a helpful resource.)*

More Resources for Myths and Legends from Around the World

Books

Cashford, Jules. *The Myth of Isis and Osiris*. Barefoot Books, 1993.

Climo, Shirley. *Stolen Thunder: A Norse Myth*. Clarion, 1994.

Delacre, Lulu. *Golden Tales: Myths, Legends, and Folktales from Latin America*. Scholastic, 1996.

Fisher, Leonard Everett. *The Gods and Goddesses of Ancient Egypt*. Holiday House, 1997.

Jaffe, Nina. *The Golden Flower: A Taino Myth from Puerto Rico*. Simon & Schuster Books for Young Readers, 1996.

Jeffrey, Madhur. *Seasons of Splendor: Tales, Myths & Legends of India*. Atheneum, 1985.

Krishnaswami, Uma. *The Broken Tusk: Stories of the Hindu God Ganesha*. Shoe String Press, 1996.

Matthews, Andrew. *Marduk the Mighty and Other Stories of Creation*. Millbrook Press, 1997.

McCaughrean, Geraldine. *The Silver Treasure: Myths and Legends of the World*. M.K. McElderry Books, 1997.

Middleton, Haydn. *Island of the Mighty: Stories of Old Britain*. Oxford University Press, 1987.

Moore, C.J. *Ishtar and Tammuz: a Babylonian Myth of the Seasons*. Kingfisher, 1996.

Ober, Hal. *How Music Came to the World: An Ancient Mexican Myth*. Houghton Mifflin, 1994.

Passes, David. *Dragons: Truth, Myth and Legend*. Artists & Writers, 1993.

Philip, Neil. *The Illustrated Book of Myths: Tales and Legends of the World*. Dorling Kindersley, 1995.

―――. *Odin's Family: Myths of the Vikings*. Orchard Books, 1996.

Pilling, Ann. *Creation: Read-Aloud Stories from Many Lands*. Candlewick Press, 1997.

Ragache, Gilles. *Lands of Mystery*. Cherrytree Press, 1995.

Roberts, Dale. *Wanari's Dreamtime: Aboriginal Myths for Children*. Art Australia, 1989.

Sola, Michele. *Angela Weaves a Dream*. Hyperion Books for Children, 1997.

Vuong, Lynette Dyer. *Sky Legends of Vietnam*. HarperCollins, 1993.

Computer Disc, Sound Cassettes

Legends of the Americas. Troll Communications, 1995. 1 computer laser optical disc. In English & Spanish Requires Mac LCII or higher or IBM 386 or faster. Includes legends from Mexico, Brazil, Peru, and Guatemala.

Stories from the Hearth. GlassWing Media, Inc., 1994. 2 sound cassettes. Includes Russian, Latin American, Spanish, Celtic, and Scottish stories.

Coyote and the Laughing Butterflies

Retold and illustrated by Harriet Peck Taylor

Summary

In ancient times, when animals could talk, Coyote and his wife lived on top of a mesa a day's journey from a salty lake. Coyote's wife asks him to go to the lake and get some salt which she needs for cooking. Coyote sets off. Tired from walking in the hot sun, coyote rests in the shade of a cactus when he reaches the valley of the big salty lake.

While coyote sleeps, many butterflies fly down to play a trick on him. They each take hold of a hair in Coyote's fur and carry him back home where his wife scolds him for not getting the salt she needs.

The next day, Coyote hurries back to the big salty lake.

Coyote is so tired that he takes a nap, and again the butterflies carry him back home. The next day, Coyote returns to the lake and fills his sack with salt. But once again, he falls asleep.

They had enjoyed tricking Coyote, but now the butterflies feel sorry for him. They pick up Coyote and his sack of salt and drop him back home. Coyote's wife uses the salt to cook a feast for them and their friends. Badger, Bobcat, Roadrunner, Rabbit, Lizard, Beaver and all the butterflies come and give thanks for the harvest.

Macmillan Books for Young Readers, 1995. 32 pp. Full-color illustrations. ISBN 0-02-788846-0

Activities

With Librarian Guidance

The most famous salt lake in the United States is the Great Salt Lake located in Utah. Ask a pair of students to research this lake. At **http://160.111.7.240/hologlobe/lae/na/greatsal.htm** and **http://eddy.media.utah.edu/medsol/UCME/g/GREATSALTLAKE.html** students will find useful information to share in an oral report.

With Classroom Teacher Guidance

1. The Tewa are a group of Pueblo Indians who lived in northern New Mexico. Check out several books from library collections and invite a group of students to research the Pueblo Indians. What are their homes like today? What do they eat? Do they have special customs? Ask the students to prepare an oral report to share with their class. Possible resources include: *Anasazi*, by Leonard Everett Fisher (Atheneum, 1997); *Pueblo Indians*, by Steven Cory (Lerner, 1996); and *The Pueblo Indians*, by Liza Burby (Chelsea Juniors, 1994).

2. Coyotes are found in every state except Hawaii. Invite a group of students to research these animals. How big are they? What do they eat? Why are they regarded as pests by some people? Ask students to prepare an oral report and share what they learn with the class. Helpful resources include: *Wild Dogs: Wolves, Coyotes and Foxes*, by Deborah Hodge, (Kids Can Press, 1997); *Wolves and Coyotes*, by Jane Parker Resnick, (Kidsbooks, 1995); and *Coyotes,* by Cherie Winner (Carolrhoda Books, 1995).

Crow Chief
A Plains Indian Story
Told and illustrated by Paul Goble

Summary

In an author's note, the reader learns that this story dates back to an early time before the Plains Indians had horses. The method used by the Plains Indians at this time in history for hunting buffalo was to drive a herd over a cliff. Much depended on the skill of the buffalo caller.

The story of Crow Chief explains that long ago all crows were white. At that time, the chief of the crows hated people and was a friend of the buffalo. When the crow chief saw hunters leaving their camp, the crow would warn the buffalo and they would run away, leaving the hunters hungry.

The Indians prayed for help, and a young man called Falling Star came to camp. He promised to help. First they brought him a buffalo robe. Then Falling Star and a young man went into a tipi painted with buffalo and talked to the buffalo spirits. Early the next morning, hidden in a robe, they joined the buffalo. When Crow Chief flew down to warn them, Falling Star caught the bird by its legs and carried it back to camp. Tied to where the tipi poles cross together, Crow Chief turned black from the smoke of the fires. He begged for pity. Falling Star released the crow. After that, crows remained black and followed behind hunters to eat pieces of meat that the hunters left for them.

Orchard Books, 1992. 32 pp. Color illustrations. ISBN 0531-05947-2

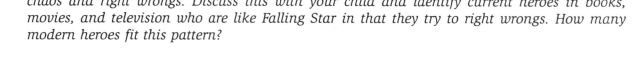

Activities

With Librarian Guidance

Many buffalo live today in Custer State Park in the Black Hills of South Dakota. Invite two students to write a letter requesting information about the buffalo. Be sure that they include a 9 x 12-inch self-addressed, stamped envelope. Allow time for the students to share any pamphlets they receive. Write to: Custer State Park, HC 83, Box 70, Custer, SD 57730. In your search for other information for your vertical file on this topic visit **http://www.state.sd.us/sdparks/custer/more.htm** and **http://thunder.state.sd.us/state/executive/tourism/sdparks/custer/custer.htm** for maps and general information.

With Classroom Teacher Guidance

The last page in the book has old songs about the crow. With the help of the music educator, have students make simple drums and play them as they chant these songs. When they have rehearsed, students might present their songs to another class.

With Parent/Caregiver Guidance

The librarian or classroom teacher might duplicate and send home the following note:

Dear Parent: Your child has read Crow Chief: A Plains Indian Story *(summary attached). In his opening notes, the author explains that Falling Star travels ceaselessly to help bring order to chaos and right wrongs. Discuss this with your child and identify current heroes in books, movies, and television who are like Falling Star in that they try to right wrongs. How many modern heroes fit this pattern?*

The Eagle's Song
A Tale from the Pacific Northwest
Adapted and illustrated by Kristina Rodanas

Summary

This tale begins by explaining that long ago people lived in huts facing the sea, but they were separated from one another by thick forests. The people never spoke with each other and did not share their supplies.

In one of the houses live three brothers. The older two are skilled hunters. The youngest brother, Ermine, carves and decorates bowls and builds boxes. One day, the hunters do not return. Ermine goes looking for them. He sees a dark spot in the sky and watches as an eagle appears and turns into a young man. Ermine soon learns that the eagle has changed his brothers into icy rivers because they tried to claim his feathers.

The eagle-man carries Ermine to mother eagle, who offers food and chides him because his people do not share. When mother eagle makes music, Ermine dances and sings. When Ermine returns home, he makes a drum, begins to play, and other children come and join him. Then men, women, animals, birds, and people from far away hear the music and feel its magic. They gather near Ermine's hut.

Ermine's brothers are released from the spell they were under and come home. From then on, instead of being isolated, people live in villages and share, and mother eagle becomes young again.

Little, Brown, 1995. 30 pp. Full-color illustrations. ISBN 0-316-75375-0

Activities

With Librarian Guidance

Ask a pair of students to research eagles. They might visit **http://www.eaglekids.com** to learn more about eagles and birds, and to take part in games and contests. A useful reference is ***Bald Eagles,*** by Karen Dudley (Raintree Steck-Vaughn, 1998). When did the eagle became a national symbol of our country? What are some places where the symbol of the eagle appears? Have these students write a report, including a bibliography, and post it on a bulletin board or on a school Web site.

With Classroom Teacher Guidance

Ermine is an interesting name for an Indian boy. Invite a pair of students to do some research in an encyclopedia. What are ermine? Where are they found? How have their furs been used? ***The World of Animals*** (Lothrop, 1998) contains excellent paintings of small animals with a brief text. Ask these students to share what they learn in an oral report to the class.

With Parent/Caregiver Guidance

The librarian or classroom teacher might duplicate the following note.

Dear Parent: You child has read The Eagle's Song *(summary attached). Working with the music educator, we will be doing Native American chants accompanied by drums in school. Could you assist your child in making a drum? Remove both ends from an empty coffee can. Cover the sides with construction paper covered in Indian designs. Cover both ends with contact paper.*

Feathers Like a Rainbow
An Amazon Indian Tale
Written and illustrated by Flora

Summary

According to this legend, long ago the birds that lived in the great rain forest around the Amazon River had dark feathers.

One young bird, Jacamin, complains to his mother, saying he wants feathers as bright as flowers. His mother, a gray-winged trumpeter, says that she will try to find colors for him.

Jacamin's mother sets off on her search. She meets up with a macaw and asks if the macaw knows where she might find colors as beautiful as the rainbow. The macaw does not know, but joins in the search. Other birds, all wanting bright colors for their feathers, join them. The birds search unsuccessfully all day.

As it is getting dark, they see a colorful hummingbird. The bird explains that it gets beautiful feathers from the flowers it visits. It takes a dab of color from each, drops the colors in a bowl, and splashes a little on its feathers.

The next day the birds try to visit colorful flowers like the hummingbird, but find they are too heavy to hover in the air and that their beaks are too big to reach inside the flowers. Jacamin's mother decides to steal the bowl of colors for her son. But before he can splash himself in colors, the others birds come and take them. All that is left is the color purple, and that is why the gray-winged trumpeter has a purple breast.

Harper & Row, 1989. 26 pp. Color illustrations. ISBN 0-06-021837-1

Activities

With Librarian Guidance

The jacket of the book explains that the writer/illustrator of this book, Flora, has contributed work to the World Wildlife Fund. Invite a pair of students to research the organization, learn when it was founded and what sort of work it does, and to report their findings orally to the class. One useful source is **http://www.wwf.org/** which gives information about the logo, the organization's activities, and describes the way in which students could be involved in a project.

With Classroom Teacher Guidance

1. Hummingbirds are also found in the United States. Ask a pair of students to research this topic using a field guide to North American birds. Which hummingbirds can be found in your state? What sorts of nests do they make? Ask these students to make an oral report on hummingbirds to the rest of the class. A useful resource is: **http://www.donaldburger.com/hbfacts.htm**. If the video, **Hummingbirds Up Close,** by the National Audubon Society (Nature Science Network, 1988) is available, this would be very informative.

2. The rain forest in this book is found along the Amazon River. Invite a group of students to research this great river. Where does it begin and end? How long is it? How does it compare in length with other great rivers? Students should consult an encyclopedia and an atlas such as **The Times Atlas of the World**. Provide time for researchers to orally present what they learn.

First Houses
Native American Homes and Sacred Structures
By Jean Guard Monroe and Ray A. Williamson
Illustrated by Susan Johnston Carlson

Summary

The authors have gathered legends associated with Native American houses and sacred structures from across the country. Included are: "The People of the Longhouse: The Iroquois League; A Gift of the Gods: The Navajo Hogan; Emergence from the Underworld: The Pueblo Kiva; Shade and Shelter: Mohave Houses; Sun's Crystal House: California House Myths; Painted Planks and Totem Poles: Northwest Coast Dwellings; Painted Tipis: House Legends of the Plains; Models of the World: Pawnee Earth Lodges; The Big House: A Delaware Ceremonial Dwelling;" and "The First Sweatlodge."

In the preface, the authors point out that Native Americans construct their traditional dwellings and sacred buildings according to cosmic patterns given by the gods. Myths involving the first houses are common throughout various groups and are usually set in the time when the earth was young and when animals, which shared human characteristics, helped to shape the world and to build the first houses.

These house stories focus on homes in temperate North America which are always constructed with local terrain in mind. The book contains a glossary, suggestions for further reading, a bibliography, and an index.

Houghton Mifflin, 1993. 150 pp. Illustrated with black and white drawings. ISBN 0-395-51081-3

Activities

With Librarian Guidance

Bandelier National Monument near Santa Fe, New Mexico, has cliff dwellings, pueblo ruins, and a ceremonial cave. Invite a student to write to the monument requesting pamphlets to share with the class. Be sure to include a stamped, self-addressed 9-x-12-inch envelope with the initial letter for use in reply. For additional information, the Great Outdoor Recreation Page, **http://www.gorp.com/gorp.resource/us_nm/nm_bande.htm** contains data on the Anasazi, ruins, what to see and do, the Tsankawi section, hiking, camping, falls, services, and photographs.

With Classroom Teacher Guidance

1. Using drawings from the book, and from other available resources, pairs of students could work together to make models of Native American houses out of simple materials. The models might be displayed in the library. Included would be an Iroquois longhouse, a Navajo hogan, a thatch Chumash house, a redwood Yurok house, a Northwest dwelling, a tipi, a Pawnee earth lodge, and a Delaware big house,

2. The Pawnee thunder ritual is held when the Pleiades appear in the right position in the smoke hole of the earth lodge. There are many stories written about the Pleiades. Invite a group of students to research this topic and share with the class some of the stories they find about this constellation.

   An Iroquois version of the story is at:
   http://discovery.syr.edu/Virtual/Lessons/crossroads/sec3/gr3/unit1/u1g314.htm.

Four Ancestors
Stories, Songs, and Poems from Native North America
Told by Joseph Bruchac • Illustrated by S.S. Burrus, Jeffrey Chapman, Murv Jacob, and Duke Sine

Summary

This book is divided into four sections, and poems and songs are scattered throughout the book. The following are included in the sections called "Fire": "Greeting the Sun, A Maushop Story" (Wampanoag), "The Moon Basket" (Pawnee), "The Three Hunters and the Great Bear" (Seneca), and "How Coyote Stole Fire" (Colville).

The second section, called "Earth," contains the following stories: "How the Earth Began" (Osage), "Wihio and Grandfather Rock" (Cheyenne), "Tacobud, The Mountain that Ate People (Nisqually), "Clay Old Woman and Clay Old Man" (Cochiti Pueblo), and "Talking to the Clay" (Catawba).

The third section, "Water," contains the following stories: "The Cloud Swallower Giant" (Zuni), "Gluskabe and the Snow Bird" (Penobscot), "Aglabem's Dam" (Maliseet), "Raven and the Tides" (Tshimshian), and "How the Prairie Became Ocean" (Yurok).

The final section, "Air," contains the following stories: "The Bird Whose Wings Made the Wind" (Micmac), "The Whirlwind Within" (Navajo), "How Saynday Tried to Marry Whirlwind Girl" (Kiowa), "How the People Pushed Up the Sky" (Snohomish), and "The Gift of Stories, The Gift of Breath" (Anenaki).

BridgeWater Books, 1996. 96 pp. Full-color illustrations. ISBN 0-8167-3843-2

Activities

With Librarian Guidance

Studying the "Water" section of this book provides a reason for students to explore your library's poetry collection for poems about clouds, rain, snow, etc. Invite a group of children to collect a number of weather poems, to make copies of them using a computer, and to display them on a Weather Poetry bulletin board in the library. If you have access to *Granger's Index to Poetry*, this would be an excellent time to introduce it.

With Classroom Teacher Guidance

1. "The Three Hunters and the Great Bear" tells about the origin of the constellation we call the Big Dipper. There are many other stories about this constellation. Ask a pair of students to locate two other stories about the Big Dipper and bring these to share to the class. Discuss what the stories have in common. Which is the class favorite? Possible resources include: ***Constellations,*** by Diane Sipiera (Children's Press, 1997) and Janice VanCleave's ***Constellations for Every Kid: Easy Activities That Make Learning Science Fun***, by Janice Pratt VanCleave (Wiley, 1997).

2. "Clay Old Woman and Clay Old Man" describes coiled clay pots. With the help of the school's art educator, introduce students to the techniques of making clay pots. If the school has a kiln, fire the pots. If it is autumn, you might go on a hike to gather dry grasses and weeds to arrange in the pots. They would make an attractive exhibit in a display case.

The Girl Who Married the Moon
Tales from Native North America
Told by Joseph Bruchac and Gayle Ross

Summary

This book contains sixteen stories that celebrate the passage from girlhood to womanhood. Among the stories of the Northeast are "Arrowhead Finger" (Penobscot), "The Abandoned Girl" (Seneca), "The Girl and the Chenoo" (Passamaquoddy), and "The Girl Who Escaped" (Mohegan).

Among the stories included from the Southeast are "Stonecoat" (Cherokee), "The Girl Who Helped Thunder" (Muskogee), "The Girl Who Married an Osage" (Piankeshaw), and "The Girls Who Almost Married an Owl" (Caddo).

The stories from the Southwest include "The Poor Turkey Girl" (Santa Clara Pueblo), "The Girl Who Gave Birth to Water-Jar Boy" (Cochiti Pueblo), "The Bear Woman" (Navajo), and "The Beauty Way—The Ceremony of White-Painted Woman" (Apache) which explains in some detail actual ceremonies held to celebrate a young girl's entrance into womanhood.

The final section on the Northwest includes "How Pelican Girl was Saved" (Lake Miwok), "Where the Girl Rescued Her Brother" (Cheyenne), "Chipmunk Girl and Owl Woman" (Okanagan), and "The Girl Who Married the Moon" (Alutiiq).

A list of source books is included.

BridgeWater Books, 1994. 127 pp. Black and white drawings. ISBN 0-8167-3480-1

Activities

With Librarian Guidance

Indian tribes of the Southwest are celebrated for their beautiful weaving. Various books and magazines will provide students with pictures of blankets and rugs. At the Web site **http://www.grantbc.com/chakra/rugs.html** you will find information and see the Diamond Red, Storm, and Classic Grey patterns. Try to locate someone in the community who collects Navajo rugs or blankets, and invite them to visit and show their collection. A local weaver's guild might be willing to demonstrate weaving techniques.

With Classroom Teacher Guidance

A small group of students might want to turn the story "The Girl Who Married the Moon" into a simple 32-page picturebook story to share with a primary grade class. The work can be divided between writers, illustrators, and readers. After the narrative has been printed using a typewriter or computer, it can be illustrated. Finally, the students can prepare a cover, bind the book, and present it to a primary grade class.

With Parent/Caregiver Guidance

The classroom teacher or librarian might want to duplicate the following letter:

Dear Parent: Your child has read The Girl Who Married the Moon: Tales from Native North America *(summary attached) and has volunteered to learn one of these stories and present it to another class as a storyteller. Allowing your child to practice his/her storytelling techniques in front of you, and giving feedback, would be very helpful.*

How Glooskap Outwits the Ice Giants and Other Tales of the Maritime Indians

Retold by Howard Norman • Illustrated by Michael McCurdy

Summary

This book contains six unusual tales, all of which involve the the giant Glooskap as the central figure. In many Indian languages this name means "man from nothing," because he is considered the first human being.

In the first story, "How Glooskap Made Human Beings," the lonely giant decides to make human beings but he worries about how they will survive, since he has already made animals that are all giants like himself. Glooskap questions and shrinks the animals to their present-day size before he finally creates humans.

In the second and third stories, "How Glooskap Outwits the Ice Giants" and "Why the Sea Winds Are the Strength They Are Today," Glooskap protects the humans he has created. In "Glooskap Gets Two Surprises," the giant throws a tantrum and has one thrown right back at him.

"How Magic Friend Fox Helped Glooskap Against the Panther-Witch" tells how Fox helped restore Glooskap as king of all the Indians. In the final story, "How Glooskap Sang through the Rapids and Found a New Home," the giant is tired of being bothered by others and seeks a quiet refuge along a river with only his wolves for company.

Little, Brown, 1989. 60 pp. Illustrated with striking wood engravings. ISBN 0-316-61181-6

Activities

With Librarian Guidance

In the story about the sea winds, Glooskap notices a whale spouting not far from shore. Invite a group of students to research whaling using print and nonprint resources. Have them write a paper about whaling, including a bibliography. At **http://160.111.7.240/resource/faq/nmnh/whaling.htm** is a bibliography from the Smithsonian on book and magazine references to whaling. *The New England Whaler,* by Robert F. Baldwin (Lerner, 1996), and *The Story of Yankee Whaling,* by the editors of the *American Heritage* are useful sources of information. An account of whale hunters at **http://outside.starwave.com/magazine/1095/10f_whal.html** was published in the Oct. 1995 issue of *Outside Magazine.*

With Classroom Teacher Guidance

1. In order to fully appreciate this set of stories, students will need to identify the setting. Using an available atlas, ask a pair of students to draw to scale a large map of the northeastern United States and Canada and on it locate Maine, Nova Scotia, and the Bay of Fundy. Post the completed map on the library bulletin board.

2. Glooskap calmed the sea winds, but our east coast still suffers from tremendous storms. Ask a small group of students to research hurricanes and then share what they learn in the form of a panel discussion. Two useful resources are Stephen P. Kramer's *Eye of the Storm: Chasing Storms* (Putnam, 1997), and Nick Arnold's *Volcano, Earthquake & Hurricane* (Wayland, 1996).

Keepers of the Night
Native American Stories and Nocturnal Activities for Children
By Michael J. Caduto and Joseph Bruchac
Illustrated by David Kanietakeron Fadden

Summary

This is a book about learning to appreciate nature at night. It contains eight Native North American stories: "The Birth of Light" (Yuchi); "How the Bat Came to Be" (Anishinabe); "Moth, the Fire Dancer" (Paiute); "Oot-Kwab-Tah, the Seven Star Dancers" (Onondaga); "The Creation of the Moon" (Dine); "Chipmunk and the Owl Sisters" (Okanagan); "The Great Lacrosse Game" (Menominee); and "How Grizzly Bear Climbed the Mountain" (Shoshone).

The first chapter is devoted to "Tips and Techniques for Bringing This Book to Life." The authors suggest that through the stories and lessons provided, teachers, parents, camp counselors and others will have the tools to bring knowledge, skills, and enjoyment to children.

In chapters 2 through 6, each story is presented and is followed by a "discussion." The story and discussion serve as springboards to activities. Various symbols are used to show whether the activity is to be carried on outdoors or indoors and whether the focus is on sensory awareness of the night world; understanding of the night world; caring for plants, animals and the environment; or caring for people.

Fulcrum, 1994. 146p. Black and white drawings. ISBN 1-55591-177-3

Activities

With Librarian Guidance

Chapter 6 focuses on bears. You may want students to investigate topics such as bears in National Parks. To begin or add to a library vertical file on this topic, ask a pair of students to write to Yellowstone Park requesting information on bears in the park. They should include a stamped, 9-x-12-inch envelope with a return address on it. Also visit Yellowstone Grizzly Journal **http://www.wyoming.com/~ygf/YGF.YGFJRNLFW95.html** and Grizzly Bear Info at **http://www.wyoming.com/~ygf/YGF.GrizInfo.html**. Students may write and share papers on bear-related topics.

With Parent/Caregiver Guidance

1. The classroom teacher should solicit two parents to serve as directors for a group of students to make and present a puppet show. Page eight shows how to make double-sided stick puppets. "Moth, the Fire Dancer," lends itself to being presented as a puppet show. Five students are needed to work the three people and three moth puppets. (One puppet shows a moth before and one after he is burned.) Props include a campfire.

2. The teacher should solicit an interested parent who is a photographer to work with a pair of students who have read "The Seven Star Dancers." On a clear night, the parent and students should load black and white film in a camera with adjustable shutter speed, mounted on a tripod, and focused on the North Star, to get a picture of star tracks to share with the class.

Old Bag of Bones
A Coyote Tale
Retold and illustrated by Janet Stevens

Summary

As the story opens, old Coyote is feeling sorry for himself. He is tired, his eyesight is failing, he's lost his teeth, and he feels like an old bag of bones. Coyote decides to ask Young Buffalo to share some of his strength, youth, and power with him. To accomplish this, Young Buffalo takes Coyote to Bear Butte and rams into him, knocking him down the butte.

When the dust clears, Coyote looks like a buffalo except for his coyote tail. Young Buffalo reminds him that though he looks like a young buffalo on the outside, on the inside he is still a powerless coyote. He calls the changed coyote a Buffote.

In turn, Buffote meets Old Rabbit, Old Lizard, and a kangaroo rat. He insists on making them young again. They protest, saying that they value age, wisdom, and experience. But Buffote carries them on his back to Bear Butte.

At Bear Butte, Buffote marches and prances and asks the others to close their eyes while he changes them forever. Then he rams them, and they all tumble down Bear Butte. The other animals do not change, but Buffote changes back into Coyote again. He is on his way to try to find food and respect with his coyote relatives when he spies a majestic elk. Quickly Coyote asks if the elk will share his youth and power with him.

Holiday House, 1996. 32 pp. Full-color illustrations. ISBN 0-8234-1215-6

Activities

With Librarian Guidance

Coyotes are controversial. Use UnCover or the *Reader's Guide to Periodical Literature* to locate recent articles about them. Also visit the Web to learn about problems in Lake Tahoe **http:/mtdemocrat.com/news/feedlaw.html.** To learn about predator poisoning see **http://www.edf.org/pubs/EDF-Letter/1975/Nov/i_poison.html.** To read about a petition from cat lovers see **http://cda.net/stories/1997/Oct.31/S300035.asp.** Invite a group of students to research this topic, and then discuss with the class problems associated with coyotes.

With Classroom Teacher Guidance

Many animals have antlers or horns. Ask a group of students to research and write a short report for the class about the headgear of one of the following: elk, moose, deer, bighorn sheep, and Rocky Mountain goat. All may be viewed at **http://www.mtn-park-lodges.com/english/wildvue.html** about wildlife in Jasper. A useful book is *Armor to Venom: Animal Defenses,* by Phyllis J. Perry (Franklin Watts, 1997).

With Parent/Caregiver Guidance

The classroom teacher or librarian might write the following letter:

Dear Parent: Your child read Old Bag of Bones *(summary attached) where Coyote turns into a combination buffalo and coyote. The assignment is to draw a combination animal and write a paragraph telling where it lives and what it eats. Your child may want to discuss with you what might make an interesting and humorous combination animal to include on a class bulletin board.*

The Rough-Face Girl

By Rafe Martin • Illustrated by David Shannon

Summary

This tale is an Algonquin Indian Cinderella story. An Invisible Being, who is said to be very great, rich, and powerful lives apart from the others in a huge wigwam. Many girls in the village want to marry him, but he is guarded by his sister who says, "Only the one who can see him can marry him."

Also living in the village is a poor man with three daughters. The two older daughters are cruel. The youngest daughter is scarred from constantly sitting by the fire to feed the flames. Her long black hair is ragged and charred.

One day the two older daughters ask their father for new buckskin robes, moccasins, and necklaces. They dress up and march through the village on their way to the wigwam of the Invisible Being. When they arrive, they cannot answer correctly the questions put by the sister. When the Invisible Being enters the wigwam where they sit, they cannot see him.

The youngest daughter goes to the Invisible Being in bark clothing, a broken shell necklace, and her father's old moccasins. The youngest daughter answers the sister's questions.

She can see the Invisible Being, and he thinks she is beautiful. The youngest daughter bathes in the lake, and her scars vanish. She marries the Invisible Being and lives happily.

G. P. Putnam, 1992. 32 pp. Full-color illustrations. ISBN 0-399-21859-9

Activities

With Librarian Guidance:

As a read-aloud, share with the class Michael Dorris's **Guests** (Hyperion, 1994), which tells the adventures of an Algonquin Indian boy and girl at the time of the first Thanksgiving. Gather available reference books on Indian tribes. Then share this student written and researched story about the Algonquin Indians of Spectacle Island, at **http://kalypso.cybercom.net/ ~ dhe/picaboan7.html**. Have the students, working individually or in groups, write original stories about the Algonquins. Allow time for sharing.

With Classroom Teacher Guidance:

1. *The Rough-Face Girl* is one of about 1,500 versions of the Cinderella story. Ask your librarian to gather different versions of Cinderella and ask students to bring copies from home, or their local public library. Interested students should form a book discussion group. After they have read several versions of the story, they can discuss them. What ideas remain central? What variations are included? Which version is most enjoyable? Why?

2. In many Cinderella stories there is a fairy godmother who helps to dress Cinderella. Invite students to write a story giving the Rough-Face Girl a fairy godmother who helps clothe her for her trip to the Invisible Being. (This godmother could be an animal, such as coyote, or it could be a spirit.) Post the stories on a bulletin board. Students may include an illustration if they wish to show how the Rough-Face Girl was dressed.

Native American Animal Stories

Told by Joseph Bruchac • Illustrated by John Kahionhes Fadden and David Kanietakeron Fadden

Summary

The contents of this book are divided into an introduction, six sections, and an afterword. An introductory map showing the location of various Native American groups is included. The introduction contains two tales, a creation myth and a hunting story. The first section, "Creation," also includes two stories, one about the Hopi and one about the people of the Osage. "Celebration" contains "The Rabbit Dance" and "The Deer Dance." "Vision" includes a Zuni tale, "Eagle Boy."

The largest section of this book, "Feathers and Fur, Scales and Skin," contains stories about a variety of creatures: "Turtle Races with Beaver, Octopus and Raven, How the Butterflies Came to Be, Salmon Boy, The Woman Who Married a Frog, How Poison Came into the World, The Boy and the Rattlesnake, The First Flute, Manabozho and the Woodpecker, Why Coyote Has Yellow Eyes, The Dogs Who Saved Their Master," and "Why Possum Has a Naked Tail."

Survival includes four stories: "How the Fawn Got Its Spots, The Alligator and the Hunter, The Gift of the Whale," and "The Passing of the Buffalo." In the afterword is the Cherokee story of "The Lake of the Wounded."

Fulcrum, 1992. 135pp. Black and white illustrations. ISBN 1-555591-127-7

Activities

With Librarian Guidance

On page 109 of this book, there is mention of Chief Seattle, who was a leader of the Duwamish League of Puget Sound. Invite a group of students to research Chief Seattle and his famous environmental speech, and ask them to write a paper to be posted on the bulletin board. They should consult **Wisdom of the Great Chiefs: The Classic Speeches of Red Jacket, Chief Joseph, and Chief Seattle,** selected by Kent Nerburn (New World Library, 1994, 76pp.). Various Web sites will help to reveal the controversy surrounding the authenticity of the speech including **http://www.synaptic.bc.ca/ejournal/wslibrry.htm.**

With Classroom Teacher Guidance

The Hopi are famous for their Kachinas. Share with the class **Kachina Dolls: The Art of Hopi Carvers,** by Helga Teiwes (University of Arizona Press, 1993) or a similar book. Visit **http://www.potcarrier.com/kachinas.html** for information and pictures about the Hopi, Kachinas, and their dances. Invite to class a guest who has a collection of these dolls and is willing to talk about them. Follow up with a student-written thank you note.

With Parent/Caregiver Guidance

Invite a parent with musical background to work with a group of students to write an original chant, similar to that included in the story "Eagle Boy," which celebrates the joy of animals flying or running. They should set a rhythm for it, using drums or other musical instruments. Ask them to practice it and record their chant on tape. When it is complete, play the tape for the class.

The Tree That Rains
The Flood Myth of the Huichol Indians of Mexico
Retold by Emery Bernhard • Illustrated by Durga Bernhard

Summary

Watakame works hard in his fields and is always accompanied by one of his five dogs. One day, Watakame returns to a field he has cleared and finds that trees have sprung up again overnight. Again he chops down the trees, but they regrow. After four days of this, Watakame hides to watch what is happening.

At sunset, a little old woman rises up out of the earth, points her bamboo staff, and all the trees in the field grow up again. The old woman explains that she is Great-Grandmother Earth. To survive the flood, she explains that Watakame should carve a boat from the fig tree, gather up certain seeds, and take refuge in the boat with the dog.

The flood comes and the boat drifts for five years. Then the waters drop. Watakame and his dog get out of the boat and plant seeds. The next day, things are growing and water gushes from the leaves of the fig tree, watering the fields.

Watakame lives in a cave and finds food ready every night. He hides and sees a small woman take off the dog's skin and start to cook. Watakame burns the skin and takes the woman for his wife. They and their children live happily together.

Holiday House, 1994. 32 pp. Color illustrations. ISBN 0-8234-1108-7

Activities

With Librarian Guidance

Introduce primary students to the library's collection of globes, atlases and maps. Help them to project, using an opaque projector, a map of Mexico onto a large sheet of white paper and trace its outline. Invite the students to consult the map of Mexico they found in the atlas and to locate and add to their map the Sierra Madre Mountains, Mexico City, and Lake Chapala.

With Art Teacher Guidance

Share this book with your art educator. The book jacket explains the illustrator is interested in the unique use of color and tone found in Huichol yarn paintings and textiles. If your library does not have a copy of **Huichol Indian Sacred Rituals** containing painting by Mariano Valadez with captions by Susana Valadez, (Amber Lotus, 1992, 1997) with examples of these yarn paintings, borrow one through interlibrary loan. Use both books to show students this unique art form.

With Parent/Caregiver Guidance

The classroom teacher could send home a note to parents asking for volunteers to help with a cooking project to take place during a specific school week. Tortillas are frequently mentioned in this story. If there is a kitchen in the school that could be used, and with sufficient parent volunteers to assist and work with a student committee, a Mexican lunch of tortillas and beans could be shared. Shopping, determining quantities needed, cooking and serving should be done primarily by the students.

They Dance in the Sky
Native American Star Myths
By Jean Guard Monroe and Ray A. Williamson

Summary

Native Americans had no written language so they depended on master storytellers to transmit their ideas orally. Their folklore and mythology are filled with tales about the natural world and how humans relate to it. Many of these stories tell about the "Beginning Time" when animals could talk and when people could change into animal shapes and back again with ease.

This book contains eight stories: "Seven Dancing Stars, The Celestial Bear, Coyote Scatters the Stars, When Stars Fell to Earth, Morning Star, They Live in the Sky, Chinook Wind," and "Star Beings." The commentary in each section explains about the culture and the world view of the peoples who told these stories. There is a glossary and bibliography.

The first two chapters contain short stories which come from different Indian tribes telling about the Pleiades and the Big Dipper. For example, in "Seven Dancing Stars" there are four legends about the Pleiades. These legends come from the Onondaga, the Shasta Indians, the Monache Indians, and the Tachi Yokuts. The remaining chapters present sky stories in a regional context to promote an understanding of the cultures from which the tales derive. Where possible, the star patterns are identified by constellation names from the Western tradition.

Houghton Mifflin, 1987. 130 pp. Black and white illustrations. ISBN 0-395-39970-X

Activities

With Classroom Librarian Guidance

Many students will be interested in astronomy. You might invite them to visit **http://www.phy.ilstu.edu/planet.html** which is the Illinois State University Planetarium Home Page. It contains a list of favorite astronomy URLs which students can explore. Another site, **http://www.skypub.com/** is Sky On Line, Your Astronomy Source on the World Wide Web. Let students work in pairs and choose a topic from the URLs to investigate further such as Space Station Mir, comets, meteors, telescopes, the next eclipse, etc. Copies of astronomy magazines such as *Astronomy Magazine* and *Sky and Telescope Magazine* will add to the information resources. If there is a planetarium in your area, plan a class field trip.

With Classroom Teacher Guidance

A falling star draws our attention today just as it did years ago to Native Americans. Have students write their own legends to explain a falling star. They might want to reread the story "Bright Shining Old Man" and review that explanation. The finished stories might be gathered together into a class book and placed in the school library or on a school Web site.

With Music Teacher Guidance

Share this book with your music educator. One group of Pawnee, the Skidi, mentioned in chapter four of this book, esteemed the planets as well as stars. Have the school music educator play "The Planets" by Gustav Holst for your class and discuss the music. They may wish to draw as they listen. What moods do various sections evoke? Which sections do students enjoy most?

White Wolf Woman
Native American Transformation Myths
Collected and retold by Teresa Pijoan

Summary

This is a collection of Native American transformation myths. Section 1, "Snakes," contains nine stories: "Thunder Son" (Algonquin), "Spirit Eggs" (Cheyenne), "Snake-Boy" (Cherokee), "Water Monster Snake-Man" (Chiricahua Apache), "Rattlesnake Father" (Pomo), "Woman Seeker" (Hopi),"Water Jar Boy" (Sikyatki), "Sacred Snake" (Zuni), and "Greedy Brothers" (Brule Sioux).

Section 2, "Wolves," contains eight stories: "Ghost Hunter" (Dakota), "White Wolf Woman" (Zuni), "Wolf-Chief's Son" (Tlingit), "Three Mountain Wolf-Water Monster" (Chiricahua), "Wolf Star" (Pawnee), "Wolf Woman Running" (Sioux), "Medicine Wolf" (Blackfoot), and "Wolf Daughter" (Eskimo).

Section 3, "Bears," contains seven stories: "The Boy and the Bear" (Iroquois), "Bear-Mother" (Haida), "Bear Songs" (Cherokee), "Beast Bear Man" (Guiana), "Bearskin-Woman" (Blackfoot), "Bear-Man" (Pawnee), and "Ma'nabush and the Bear" (Menomini).

Section 4, "Other Animals," contains thirteen stories: "Porcupine vs. Thunderers" (Iroquois), "White Hawk" (Shawnee), "Seneca Medicine" (Seneca), "Devilfish Promise" (Haida), "First People" (Eskimo), "Gopher's Wisdom" (Sioux), "Wolf Clan Lesson" (Nass River People), "KoKo Wisdom" (Zuni), "Faithless Woman" (Iroquois), "Monkey-Wife" (Guiana), "Miqka'no, Turtle Chief" (Miqka'no) and "Magic Beasts" (Comanche).

August House, 1992. 167 pp. ISBN 0-87483-200-4

Activities

With Librarian Guidance

The grey wolf is now very scarce in New Mexico. Ask a group of students to research endangered wolves. They should use the *Reader's Guide to Periodical Literature* or a computerized periodical index, if one is available in their library. They can then arrange to locate the articles on the topic in the library's magazine collection, or use a computer service that furnishes the full text of the articles. Other resources include: **http://icdweb.cc.purdue.edu/ ~ andri/wolves/page3.html** which offers current data about endangered wolves and **http://www.defenders.org/lobomyth.html** which gives a series of myths and facts concerning the Mexican wolf. Students should make a presentation to the class on what they learn.

With Classroom Teacher Guidance

1. The stories in this book represent 30 Native American tribes. Ask a pair of students to prepare a map using an opaque projector to project the outline of North America on a large piece of paper so they can trace it. Using available reference books, they should locate each of the tribes mentioned. On the map, they should list each of the tribes in their correct geographical area. Post the map on a bulletin board.

2. In the introduction to Bears, sandpainting is discussed. Someone in your community may have a sand painting and know something of its history. Invite that person to visit the class with the painting and share information about it. A useful resource for adults is *The Navajo Art of Sandpainting*, by Douglas Congdon-Martin (Schiffer, 1990).

The Woman Who Fell from the Sky
The Iroquois Story of Creation
Retold by John Bierhorst • Illustrated by Robert Andrew Parker

Summary

The author has written several other books on Native American lore including *In the Trail of the Wind, The Girl Who Married a Ghost, Spirit Child,* and *The Naked Bear: Folktales of the Iroquois,* all of which were named Notable Books by the American Library Association.

According to the Iroquois creation story, sky people lived on a floating island in the air where light came from the flowers of a tall tree. No one ever died, and no one new was ever born.

One of the sky people tells her husband that she will be the mother of children. Her husband grows angry, uproots the light-giving tree, and pushes his wife through the hole.

Sky people turn into ducks and cushion her fall. Others turn into water animals. A muskrat dives, brings up mud, and spreads it on the back of a turtle. Sky Woman walks around on the turtle's back until the earth is as large as it is today.

The Sky Woman creates the stars, the sun, and gives birth to gentle Sapling and to Flint, who is as hard as stone. Sapling creates trees, birds, and animals. When Flint creates monsters, Sapling drives them underground. Flint creates snow, but Sapling adds spring. Sapling creates humans and teaches them how to make houses and build fires. Then the Sky Woman and her two sons return to the sky.

William Morrow, 1993. 30 pp. Full-color illustrations. ISBN 0-688-10680-3

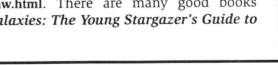

Activities

With Librarian Guidance

Sky woman lands on the back of a turtle. Invite a group of students to research and find out what are the largest species of turtles or tortoises living today. Ask the students to share with the class what they learn. Useful resources include: **Turtles,** by Anita Baskin-Salzberg (Franklin Watts, 1996), and **The Turtle and Tortoise,** by Edith Hope Fine (Crestwood, 1988). Visit **http://www.tortoise.org/geninfo.html** on care and conservation including an interviews with Dr. Michael Klemens, and **http://fovea.retina.net/ ~ gecko/herps/turtles/index.html.**

With Classroom Teacher Guidance

1. The story of the Sky Woman and the creation of the world belongs to six Indian nations: Mohawk, Oneida, Onondaga, Cayuga, Seneca, and Tuscarora. All these Iroquois nations were located in New York and southern Canada. Ask students to do research using books available in the school and local libraries and then locate on a blank map where these native peoples lived.

2. According to the story, Sapling and Flint took separate paths when they rose up from earth and traveled along the Milky Way. Ask a group of students to research the Milky Way and write a brief report to be posted on the library bulletin board. To gather information on the galaxy see **http://seds.lpl.arizona.edu/messier/more/mw.html.** There are many good books including: John R. Gustafson's **Stars, Clusters and Galaxies: The Young Stargazer's Guide to the Galaxy** (J. Messner, 1992).

More Resources for Native American & Early Indian Myths and Tales

Books

Belting, Natalia M. *Moon Was Tired of Walking On Air: Origin Myths of South American Indians.* Houghton Mifflin, 1992.

Caldwell, E.K. *Animal Lore & Legend--Bear: American Indian Legends.* Scholastic, 1996.

Cohlene, Terri. *Turquoise Boy: A Navajo Legend.* Rourke Corp., 1990.

Delacre, Lulu. *Golden Tales: Myths, Legends, and Folk Tales from Latin America.* Scholastic Press, 1996.

Dominic, Gloria. *Song of the Hermit Thrush: An Iroquois Legend.* Rourke Corp., 1996.

Goble, Paul. *Iktomi and the Buffalo Skull.* Orchard Books, 1991.

Hadley, Eric. *Legends of the Sun and Moon.* Cambridge University Press, 1990.

Harper, Piers. *How the World Was Saved & Other Native American Tales.* Western, 1994.

Hodge, Gene Meany. *Kachina Tales from the Indian Pueblos.* Sunstone Press, 1993.

Hull, Robert. *Native North American Stories.* Thomson Learning, 1993.

Lavitt, Edward. *Nihancan's Feast of Beaver: Animal Tales of the North American Indians.* Museum of New Mexico Press, 1990.

Mayo, Gretchen. *Big Trouble for Tricky Rabbit!* Walker, 1994.

———. *Earthmaker's Tales: North American Indian Stories About Earth Happenings.* Walker, 1989.

———. *Here Comes Tricky Rabbit.* Walker, 1994.

———. *Star Tales: North American Indian Stories About the Stars.* Walker, 1987.

Medicine Crow, Joseph. *From the Heart of the Crow Country: The Crow Indians' Stories.* Orion, 1992.

Midge, Tiffany. *Animal Lore & Legend--Buffalo: American Indian Legends.* Scholastic, 1995.

Troughton, Joanna. *Who Will Be the Sun? A North American Folk-Tale.* P. Bedrick Books, 1986.

Wolf, Bernard. *Beneath the Stone: A Mexican Zapotec Tale.* Orchard Books, 1994.

Young, Ed. *Moon Mother.* HarperCollins, 1993.

Audio and Video Cassettes

Octopus Lady and Crow: And Other Animal People Stories of the Northwest Coast. Society for the Study of Myth and Tradition, 1994. 1 sound cassette, 60 min. Tales of Indians of North American told by Johnny Moses.

Wolves. National Audubon Society & TBS Productions. 1 videocassette, 60 min. Describes wolves and the dangers they face today.

The Acorn Tree and Other Folktales

Retold and illustrated by Anne Rockwell

Summary

"The Acorn Tree," adapted from a Russian story, tells of an old man and old woman who live in the forest with a rooster and a magical grinding mill. In "The Thirsty Crow," a retelling of a fable from Aesop, a clever crow uses his wits to get a drink of water from a pitcher. An animal fable from India features "The Scared Little Rabbit" who believes that the earth is caving in.

An African folktale is the basis for "The Flower Children" in which a woman acquires and then loses a family. "Owl Feathers," a Puerto Rican tale, explains why the owl never comes out in the daytime. "The Greedy Cat" is a cumulative Scandinavian tale, while "The Puppy-Boy," adapted from the Inuits, explains how the good deeds of an Eskimo man and woman win them a loyal son who provides for them.

"The Dog and the Wolf," a translation of one of La Fontaine's fables, teaches the value of freedom. "La-Lee-Lu," was adapted from a story included in *Folk Lore from Maryland,* and tells of a magical flock of geese. Based on a Native American tale from Cochiti Pueblo in New Mexico, the village witchman proves no match for a magical pair of twins in "The Twins From Far Away."

Greenwillow Books, 1995. 40 pp. Full-color serigraph illustrations. ISBN 0-688-10746-X

Activities

With Librarian Guidance

After reading "Owl Feathers," students may have questions about owls. Assist these primary students in learning to use the library's computerized or card catalog. How could they find other books about owls? How could they tell if the listed books were fiction or nonfiction? Two recent informative books are **Owls,** by Kevin J. Holmes (Capstone Press, 1998), and **Owl,** by Rebecca Stefoff (Benchmark, 1998).

With Classroom Teacher Guidance

"The Thirsty Crow" involves a water trick. Have students fill a bowl half-full of water. Drop a needle into it point first. It sinks. Place the needle lengthwise on the water. It sinks. Lay the needle on a 3-inch square of tissue paper. Put the tissue on the water. It floats because the surface tension of the water is greater than the force of gravity on the needle. Have students experiment with other objects, first guessing whether they will float or sink.

With Parent/Caregiver Guidance

"The Scared Little Rabbit" would make a good stick-puppet show. Invite two parents to volunteer to work with puppeteers. Students can draw the following figures and staple them to paint-stirring sticks to serve as puppets: little rabbit, big rabbit, jackal, two monkeys, tiger, elephant, and the lion. They may want to tape record their show and play the tape as they perform with the puppets in front of a kindergarten class.

The Boy Who Found the Light

Retold and illustrated by Dale De Armond

Summary

The three Eskimo folktales which are included in this book are: "The Boy Who Found the Light; The Raven and the Marmot;" and "The Doll." In these tales, animals and people dwell on equal terms and take on one another's attributes. The stories describe origins of natural phenomena like the wind and sun and convey respect between people and animals.

In the tale "The Boy Who Found the Light," Tulugac, an orphan boy, hears about the times, long ago, when the sun and moon hung in the sky. Now there is only darkness. He decides to seek the light. He finally finds the sun and the moon by an old man's house. Tulugac hurls the moon into the sky and, by changing into a raven, carries the sun back to his people.

In "The Raven and the Marmot," a raven is accused by sea birds of being a carrion eater. The raven flies inland and threatens to eat a marmot, but the quick-thinking marmot tricks raven and makes his escape.

In "The Doll," a childless wife asks her husband to carve a doll from wood. The woman dresses the doll in fur and calls it Yuguk. Yuguk becomes a real boy. When he is older, he allows animals to come through the sky wall telling the villagers to hunt these animals only for food and to treat them with respect.

Sierra Club Books, 1990. 60 pp. Illustrated with black-and-white wood engravings. ISBN 0-316-17787-3

Activities

With Librarian Guidance

Invite a group of students to research the moon's phases and share what they learn in an oral report. Some students may wish to pursue this study as a science fair project. If so, consider *Science Project Ideas About the Moon,* by Robert Gardner (Enslow, 1997). Among other sources of information are: a site to view the phases of the moon for any date and time from 1800-2199 AD at **http://tycho.usno.navy.mil/vphase.html** or practice in figuring moon phases using an Equatorial Sky Chart at **http://walt.stcloud.msus.edu/moonpForm.fcgi.**

With Classroom Teacher Guidance

1. Totems use familiar figures such as bear, raven, and eagle. Invite a small group of students to research and study photos of totems. Then they can construct and paint a totem to display in the library. The basic structure can be made from several clean, empty ice-cream tubs. A cross piece wing can be made of cardboard. Tempera paint can be used for the designs. A useful resource might be **http://www.seatrek.com/snhp.html** which shows totems at Sitka National Historical Park, and Vicki Jensen's *Carving a Totem Pole* (Henry Holt, 1996).

2. Tulugac sleeps in a snow cave. If you live in an area where it snows, ask a class member to set one thermometer on top of the snow and bury another deep in the snow. After several hours, check the thermometers. Is there any difference? Ask the student to research and explain the findings to the class.

The Curse of the Ring

By Michael Harrison • Illustrated by Tudor Humphries

Summary

This book is a retelling of the Norse Ring or Volsung saga. As the story begins, Loki, and two gods, Odin and Honir, are on a journey through Middle Earth. Loki kills an otter and when they enter a farmhouse, Hreidmar claims the dead otter is his son. Loki takes gold as blood-money from the dwarf, Andvari, who curses a golden arm-ring that Loki takes. Loki gives the gold to Hreidmar, and he and the two gods leave.

One of Hreidmar's sons, Fafnir, immediately kills him for the gold and flees. The other son, Regin, follows him to a cave and learns Fafnir has turned into a dragon. Regin seeks Sigmund to slay the dragon. When he learns Sigmund is dead, he watches over Sigmund's infant sun, Sigurd. When Sigurd grows up, Regin convinces him to slay the dragon, Fafnir, using Sigmund's mended sword. With Fafnir dead, Regin fights with Sigurd and is killed. Sigurd finds and falls in love with Brynhild and gives her the ring. Under the power of the witch Grimhild, Sigurd forgets Brynhild and marries Gudrun. Brynhild marries Gudrun's brother and brings about Sigurd's death. Then Brynhild kills herself and joins Sigurd in death. In the days following, Gudrun's second husband, Atli, kills her two brothers, Gudrun slays Atli, and then drowns herself, leaving the cursed ring in the sea.

Oxford University Press, 1987. 80 pp. Color and black and white illustrations. ISBN 0-19-274131-4

Activities

With Librarian Guidance

Odin is mentioned throughout this story. Ask an interested group of students to research the Norse gods and to make a chart to display on a bulletin board sharing what they learn. They can find a list of Norse gods and information on the nine worlds as well as other Norse mythology links at **http://www.jmu.edu/english/myth/norse.htm**. The classic, **D'Aulaires' Norse Gods and Giants,** by Ingri D'Aulaire (Doubleday, 1967) as well as the recent **Odin's Family: Myths of the Vikings,** by Neil Philip (Orchard Books, 1996) would be good sources of information.

With Classroom Teacher Guidance

The most famous dragon stories involve Saint George. Invite a group of students to use the library's catalog to locate books about Saint George, and list titles, authors, and call numbers. Make as many of these books available for student reading as possible. Have these students hold a book discussion on Saint George when they have completed their reading.

With Parent/Caregiver Guidance

The librarian or classroom teacher might send home the following letter:

Dear Parent: Your child has read The Curse of the Ring *(summary attached). In that story, Gudron is forced to invite her brothers to come to Atli's house where she knows they will be in danger. She tries to include a warning in her message. Her warning fails. Discuss with your child what Gudron might have written that would have succeeded in warning her brothers.*

Favorite Folktales From Around the World

Edited by Jane Yolen

Summary

This book is a rich resource for teachers seeking different types of folktales. The first section, "Telling Tales," contains riddle tales. In "The Very Young and the Very Old," babies and the oldest members of society appear so innocent and clear-sighted that they seem wise.

In the tales which make up "True Loves and False," the consequences of love are explored. A trickster, playing his ingenious tricks out to the very end, is at the heart of the stories included in "Trickster, Rogues, and Cheats."

In "The Fool: Numbskulls and Noodleheads," there are stories which celebrate foolish behavior. In the tales included in "Heroes: Likely and Unlikely," the central figures outwit, outfight, and outmaneuver their opponents. The stories included in "Wonder Tales: Tall Tales and Brag," often contain bragging and outright lies.

In the "Shape Shifters," the tales deal with those who change into other creatures. "Not Quite Human" contains stories about fairies and trolls. "Fooling the Devil" contains tales about a gullible devil. The tales in "The Getting of Wisdom" comment on the many faces of wisdom. "Ghosts and Revenants" contains ghost legends. The final section, "Death and the World's End," contains stories about mortality.

Pantheon Books, 1986. 498 pp. No illustrations. ISBN 0-394-54382-3

Activities

With Librarian Guidance

The stories in this book come from all over the world. On a worksheet, number and list all the countries from which the stories come. Duplicate and give each student a blank map of the world. Ask them to place the numbers for each country in the correct spot on their map. Ask students to work individually on this task. You will need to make available the library's collection of atlases, maps, and globes. If you wish, the assignment could be self-checking by providing a completed map against which students could check their finished work.

With Classroom Teacher Guidance

In the story "Being Greedy Chokes Anansi," a witch decrees that anyone who says the word "five" will die. A guinea fowl gets food by tricking Anansi. Invite students to pick a common word and then to see if the members of the class can get through the entire day without saying it aloud. Have the students report on their success or lack of it at the end of the school day.

With Parent/Caregiver Guidance

The librarian or classroom teacher might send home the following letter.

Dear Parent: Your child has read Favorite Folktales From Around the World *(summary attached) and has volunteered to learn one of them and tell it in a primary grade classroom. As your child rehearses to present the folktale, it would be of great help if you would listen and provide feedback on techniques that might make the telling more interesting or exciting.*

Folk Stories of the Hmong
People of Laos, Thailand and Vietnam
By Norma J. Livo & Dia Cha

Summary

In the section on the Hmong and their culture, the reader learns about the history of the Hmong and their traditional beliefs and customs. The second section of the book deals with Hmong folk arts including jewelry, clothing, flower cloth, and storycloths.

The second half of the book contains a variety of Hmong folk stories, including: "The Beginning of the World, Legend of the Rice Seed, The Origin of the Shaman, Another Age of Happiness," and "Creation, Flood, Naming Story."

Another section entitled "Why Folk Stories" includes: "Why Monkey and Man Do Not Live Together, Why Animals Cannot Talk, Why People Eat Three Meals a Day and Why Doodle Bugs Roll Balls of Dung, Why Farmers Have to Work So Hard, Why Birds Are Never Hungry, Why Hmong Are Forbidden to Drink Mother's Milk, Why the Hmong Live on Mountains, Shoa and His Fire," and "The Story of the Owl."

The largest section, stories of Love, Magic and Fun, includes twelve more folk stories about couples, sisters-in-law, husbands, wives, and orphans. There is a useful bibliography.

Libraries Unlimited, 1991. 135 pp. Color illustrations showing native dress, art and textile designs.
ISBN 0-87287-854-6

Activities

With Librarian Guidance

Several of the Hmong stories feature tigers. Invite a small group of students to research Bengal tigers and to write a short paper including a bibliography. They may wish to obtain information on conservation at **http://www.5tigers.org/bengal.htm** where they can read about organizations, articles, editorials, and find additional links. To learn more about white tigers, try **http://www.5tigers.org/white2.htm** for an essay by Ronald Tilson. Useful books include *Tigers,* by Lesley A. DuTemple (Lerner, 1996), and *Tigers,* by Amanda Harman (Benchmark Books, 1996.)

With Classroom Teacher Guidance

Depending on the size of your city or town, you may have several Hmong families living in your community. If so, and if one has a storycloth (pandau), invite that person to come in and explain to students what story the stitchery records. Be sure to have students follow up with a thank you letter.

With Parent/Caregiver Guidance

The librarian or classroom teacher might duplicate the following letter:

Dear Parent: Your child has read Folk Stories of the Hmong *(summary attached) and has volunteered to learn one of the stories to present to a primary grade class as a flannelboard story. Students will make simple figures from pellon (a fabric interfacing) to place on a flannel board (provided by the school) as the story is told. It would be very helpful if you would serve as audience and provide feedback as your child practices telling the folktale.*

Ghosts, Vampires, and Werewolves
Eerie Tales from Transylvania

By Mihai I. Sparlosu and Dezso Benedek • Illustrated by Laszlo Kubinyl

Summary

The stories in this book often contain violence and do not usually end happily. These sixteen spooky stories are divided into three sections. Part One: "Ghosts, Vampires, and Werewolves" contains "The White Cross, The Forest, The Bitang, The Jealous Vampire," and "Special Delivery." In these stories, some of the ghosts and spirits that inhabit Transylvania are introduced.

Part Two: "Haunted Treasures" contains "The Three Partners, The Gypsy Fiddlers, The Female Snake, The Six-Fingered Hand, The Red Rose," and "The Ancient Fortress." Many of these stories are about spirits that are said to guard the fabulous treasures which supposedly are hidden all around the country. It also includes stories about gold mines and the spirits which inhabit them.

Part Three: "Eerie Fairy Tales" contains "The Dark Stranger, The Red Emperor's Son, The Wheel of Fire, The Wicked Queen," and "The Stone Statue." The stories in this final section contain familiar fairytale elements such as princesses, castles, and magic, but many of these also have rather gruesome endings.

There is also an introduction, as well as notes about the stories, and suggestions for further reading.

Orchard Books, 1994. 104 pp. Black and white illustrations. ISBN 0-531-06860-9

Activities

With Librarian Guidance

On hearing the name "Transylvania," students may think of Count Dracula, a character made famous by Irish writer, Bram Stoker. Ask two students to first research this author and then to make an oral report to the class sharing their information. In addition to using an encyclopedia, this would be a good time to introduce biographical references such as **Webster's** or **Chamber's Biographical Dictionary** or the **McGraw Hill Encyclopedia of World Biography**. Able readers might consult the adult book **Bram Stoker: A Biography of the Author of Dracula,** by Barbara Belford (Knopf, 1996, 381 pp.).

With Classroom Teacher Guidance

1. In "The Red Emperor's Son," Peter tries to find a place where there is no old age and death. A famous explorer, Ponce de Leon, also looked for a "fountain of youth." Ask two students to research this explorer and to give an oral report to the class sharing what they learn about him and his travels. Useful resources are Sean Dolan's **Juan Ponce de Leon,** (Chelsea House, 1995) and Wyatt Blassingame's **Ponce de Leon** (Chelsea House, 1991).

2. In the story, "The Female Snake," the snake is kind and helpful. Ask students to choose some other creature that is often feared by humans and write an adventure story in which the feared creature comes to the rescue. Allow time for those who wish to share their stories with the class.

More Stories to Solve
Fifteen Folktales from Around the World
Told by George Shannon • Illustrated by Peter Sis

Summary

In each of the fifteen folktales in this collection, there is a riddle to be solved. In "The Snowman," three boys put three big snowballs together by building a ramp. A deer solves a challenge where bigger animals fail in "The New Prince." With the help of a girl, the Kashmir's son uses one coin in a way that surprises him. In "Firefly and the Apes," one small firefly gets the better of one hundred apes. Hard swimming saves a frog from drowning in "The Frog." The Devil is outsmarted in "The Lawyer and the Devil." A traveling preacher solves a robbery in "Crowing Kettles." Aesop proves too clever for King Nactanabo in "Never Seen Never Heard." In "The Brahman and the Banker," a clever plan allows money to be recovered. Carmelita proves cleverer than her husband in "A Last Request." "Outwitting the King" is not difficult for a poor student. A frog and a deer make a bet in "Sunrise." A trick involving tall tales backfires in "The Tallest Tale." In "The Bet," the reader learns that two bets are better than one. And "The Ship" mystery is unsolved.

The basic plots of these stories come from Korea, Liberia, the Philippines, Russia, England, the United States, India, Chile, Ethiopia, Mexico, Burma, and ancient Greece.

Greenwillow Books, 1990. 64 pp. Black and white illustrations. ISBN 0-688-09161-X

Activities

With Librarian Guidance

Using the library's catalog or **www.Amazon.com,** ask two students to compile a list of other books of riddles, giving the title, author, publisher. If they use the library catalog, have them add the call number. Post their list on a bulletin board for other interested students to consult. Ask two students to maintain a "riddle bulletin board" for a month. Other students may give them original riddles and answers. The two students in charge should post original riddles on a bulletin board, supply the answers, and change the riddles each week.

With Classroom Teacher Guidance

It is interesting to compare a folktale from one country with a similar tale from another country. Ask a pair of students to read "A Last Request." Then have them find a very similar story in one of the many editions of *The Complete Grimm's Fairy Tales.* After they have compared the two stories, have the students make an oral report to the class explaining how the tales, one from Germany and one from Chile, are similar and different.

With Parent/Caregiver Guidance

The classroom teacher or librarian might duplicate the following note:

Dear Parent: Your child has read More Stories to Solve *(summary attached). In "All for One Coin," a young man buys a watermelon which gives him, his father, and the cow something to eat and drink, and seeds to plant in the garden. Discuss this story with your child. Besides another melon, can your child think of something else which would meet the father's demand? What?*

Older Brother, Younger Brother
A Korean Folktale

Retold by Nina Jaffe • Illustrations by Wenhai Ma

Summary

Two brothers live with their elderly father in a house on a mountainside. Nolbu, the older, is cruel and greedy. Hungbu, the younger, is kind, caring, and respectful. When the brothers grow up, marry, and have children, they all live together.

When the aged father dies, Nolbu tells his younger brother to leave. Hungbu and his wife and three children find an empty shack. No owners come, so they move in and start a garden in the field.

One day, Hungbu finds a swallow with a broken wing and nurses it to health. The swallow returns in spring and drops three seeds in Hungbu's hand. Hungbu plants and tends them.

Three gourds grow. One contains silk and golden coins. Another holds rice. Carpenters came out of the third gourd and build the family a magnificent new house.

Nolbu comes to see his rich brother and learns about the swallow. He finds a swallow's nest, knocks a bird out, breaks its wing, and carelessly tends it until the swallow is well enough to fly away. In the spring, this swallow brings three seeds which grow into gourds but contain mud, manure, snakes, scorpions, spiders and evil spirits that destroy his house.

Nolbu goes to his brother and begs forgiveness. Hungbu welcomes him and they all live harmoniously together.

Viking, 1995. 32 pp. Watercolor illustrations. ISBN 0-670-85645-2

Activities

With Librarian Guidance

Nolbu destroys a swallow's nest. One place where swallows are especially famous is at the Mission of San Juan Capistrano in California. Invite two students to research this topic to find out more about the birds and to write a short paper including a bibliography of their sources of information. Useful information is found in Nancy Lemke's **Missions of the Southern Coast** (Lerner, 1996) and at **http://www.pressanykey.com/missions/** which provides links to all the California missions, as well as at **http://www.missionsjc.com/** which contains information about San Juan Capistrano and the "Legend of the Swallows."

With Classroom Teacher Guidance

1. This book shows a picture of the Korean symbols for the brothers' names. Invite someone in the community who writes in Korean, Japanese, or Chinese to come to class and write and discuss the symbols that are used in their written language. If there is time, students might enjoy learning to draw certain symbols for familiar words.

2. A swallow's nest is very different from that of a robin. Invite a pair of students to find pictures of six different kinds of birds and their nests. Provide time for the students to share what they learn about birds' nests with the class. Resources include: Patricia Demuth's **Cradles in the Trees: The Story of Bird Nests** (Macmillan, 1994), and **Bird**, by David Burnie (Knopf, 1988).

Reynard the Fox

Retelling by Selina Hastings • Illustrated by Graham Percy

Summary

The story begins with angry animals who had been injured by Reynard the Fox demanding justice from the Lion, King of the Beasts. Reynard's nephew, Grimbard the Badger, tries to defend his uncle.

The king summons Reynard to appear before him. Bruin takes the message to Reynard's castle but is immediately tricked. When Bruin fails to bring Reynard, the king sends Tibert the Cat to summon Reynard. Tibert is also tricked, so the king sends Grimbard to summon Reynard. Grimbard returns to the king with his uncle the next morning. All the animals rush into court. The lion declares Reynard guilty and condemns him to be hanged.

Reynard asks to make a confession. Then he tells a story about having a great treasure. The king pardons Reynard in exchange for the treasure and plans a banquet to celebrate honoring Reynard. Halfway through the banquet, animals begin to arrive telling of new injustices committed by Reynard.

Before the king can attack, Reynard returns to court and offers to fight to show his innocence. Isegrim, the wolf, volunteers to fight him. Reynard's aunt covers him in oil so that he is slippery, and Reynard wins the fight, is reinstated in the king's favor, and returns home to his wife and cubs.

Tambourine Books, 1990. 76 pp. Full-color illustrations. ISBN 0-688-09949-1

Activities

With Librarian Guidance

1. Reynard the Fox is both cunning and a great hunter. Have three groups of students research the red fox, desert fox, and arctic fox. Ask them to share what they learn about these different animals. Resources include: **http://arnica.csustan.edu/esrpp/Sjkfprof.htm** about kit foxes; **http://www.floodlight-findings.com/2redfox/fennecfox.html** for fennec foxes; and arctic fox information at **http://www.nps.gov/bela/html/foxes.htm**. If available, students might also search in *Encyclopedia of Mammals* (Facts On File, 1995), or *Endangered Wildlife of the World* (11 vol. set, Marshall Cavendish, 1993). Other useful books are Caroline Arnold's *Fox* (Morrow, 1996), Kathy Darling's *Arctic Babies* (Walker, 1997), and Lynn M. Stone's *Desert Animals at Night* (Rourke, 1997).

With Classroom Teacher Guidance

1. In the author's introduction, she mentions William Caxton, a fifteenth century English printer. A pair of students might research Caxton in an encyclopedia to find out more about him. As a read-aloud, the teacher might share either of the following books with the class, both of which feature Caxton as one of the characters. *The Cargo of the Madalena*, by Cynthia Harnett (Lerner, 1984) or *Blood and Roses*, by Bernice Grohskopf (Atheneum, 1979).

2. Badgers are interesting animals. Ask a pair of students to research this topic and share what they learn. They might read *Badgers,* by Joan Kalbacken (Children's Press, 1996) and *Badgers,* by Lynn M. Stone (Rourke Press, 1995).

South and North, East and West

Edited by Michael Rosen • Twenty-five different illustrators

Summary

There are 25 stories in this book: "The Man Who Gave People Things to Look After" (Cyprus), "Fox Alligator, and Rabbit" (Jamaica), "The Hook" (England), "Teeth" (Jamaica), "The Cliff" (Malta), "The Daughter" (Vietnam), "Story Time" (England), "Mansoor and the Donkey" (North Africa), "The Strongest Person in the World" (Korea), "Dog, Cat, and Monkey" (Indonesia), "Hare, Hippo, and Elephant" (Central, Southern, and East Africa), "Why Do Dogs Chase Cars?" (Northern Ghana, Mauritania), "The Beginning of History" (Brazil), "Sunkaissa, The Golden-Haired Princess" (Nepal), "Ears, Eyes, Legs, and Arms" (Mali), "The Lion and the Hare" (Botswana), "The Four Brothers" (India), "The Wild Pigs" (Greece), "Snake, Horse and Toad" (West Africa), "Good Morning" (Bangladesh), "Pedro and His Dog" (Bolivia), "The Little Green Frog" (The Dominican Republic), "The Greedy Father" (Zimbabwe), "The Painter and the Judge" (China), and "A Story for a Princess" (The Middle East).

At the back of the book, there are notes about each of the stories as well as a brief discussion and history of Oxfam and the work that organization has done throughout the world during its 50-year history.

Walker Books, 1992. 95 pp. Full-color illustrations. ISBN 0-7445-2193-9

Activities

With Librarian Guidance

Make whatever atlases you have (such as *The Times Atlas of the World* or *The International Atlas*) available to the class. Using a blank world map, ask a group of students to locate and label the countries from which these stories come: Cyprus, Jamaica, England, Malta, Vietnam, North Africa, Central Africa, West Africa, South Africa, Korea, Indonesia, Ghana, Mauritania, Brazil, Nepal, Mali, Botswana, India, Greece, Bangladesh, Bolivia, the Dominican Republic, Zimbabwe, and China. Post the completed map in the library.

With Classroom Teacher Guidance

Printed on the book's cover is a statement "all royalties to benefit Oxfam." Oxfam works in over 70 countries providing food, relief, and literacy projects. Ask a pair of students to write to the U.S. address in the book for materials (including a stamped, 9 x 12-inch self-addressed envelope) and to share what information they receive with the class.

With Parent/Caregiver Guidance

The teacher could recruit a parent volunteer through a home-school newsletter to work with a small group of students to make puppets, rehearse a show, and present it to one or more classes of students in the school. "Hare, Hippo and Elephant" might be a good choice requiring only three puppets and a rope for a prop. Students could pre-record the dialogue using a tape recorder or speak their parts as they work the puppets.

Spanish-American Folktales

By Teresa Pijoan De Van Etten • Illustrated by Wendell E. Hall

Summary

A short history as to where and when the author first heard each story is included at the back of this collection, which contains 28 stories: "Leaf Monster, Lizard, The Shoes, Magician Flea, The Two Friends, Witches, River Man, Chicken Dinner, The Mare, Owl Wishes, Leticia's Turtle, Wise Stones, Meadowlark, The Wooden Horse, The River, The Flea, Remember, The Prayer, The Three Sisters and Luck, The Sheepskin, Postman, Eyes That Come Out at Night, The Mule, The Ant, The Animals' Escape, The Dispute, The Mountain Lion and the Mouse," and "The Dead One Fell."

The tales included are varied and illustrate many aspects of the culture. Some like "The River" and "Chicken Dinner" tell of the simple life of villagers and travelers. Others, such as "The Mule" involve the supernatural. Still others, such as "Leaf Monster," have wise or clever animals as the main characters. Many involve tricks being played on others such as "The Lizard" and "River Man." Some, such as "The Magician Flea" and "Witches" involve magic, while "The Mare" is an example of a humorous tale. "The Sheepskin" and "The Wooden Horse" reflect upon generations of wood carvers and shepherds.

August House, 1990. 127 pp. Black and white illustrations. ISBN 0-87483-155-5

Activities

With Librarian Guidance

Ask a pair of students to draw a large outline map of the state of New Mexico. On it, they should place in the correct locations the following spots mentioned in the stories: Santa Clara Pueblo, Santa Fe, Cuyamungue, Chilili, Las Tablas, Tres Piedra, El Mundo, Comanche Gap, El Macho, Nambe, San Juan, Alcade, Las Truchas, Chimayo, Las Cruces, Lyden, Chama, and Chupadera. A detailed map of New Mexico, such as those provided through the AAA Automobile Club would be a helpful resource. Post the finished map on a bulletin board.

With Classroom Teacher Guidance

"The Animal's Escape" is similar in some respects to "The Bremen Town Musicians." After students have read "The Animal's Escape," read to them a version of "The Bremen Town Musicians." Hold a class book discussion to compare and contrast these two stories. How are they alike? How do they differ? Which tale do students prefer, and why?

With Parent/Caregiver Guidance

The teacher might recruit a parent volunteer to work with a small student drama group. "The Ant" is a short story with only three characters. It teaches about good manners and industry. Three students, and their drama couch, might enjoy making simple costumes, rehearsing, and presenting this play to a kindergarten class. The three students might lead the kindergartners in a short discussion after the play.

Thirty-Three Multicultural Tales to Tell

By Pleasant DeSpain • Illustrated by Joe Shlichta

Summary

This book is designed for parents, educators, and storytellers. It includes: "Old Joe & the Carpenter" (United States), "The Tug of War" (Africa), "The Listening Cap" (Japan), "Rabbit's Last Race" (Mexico), "Alexander, the Dwarf & the Troll" (Denmark), "Señor Rattlesnake Learns to Fly" (Mexico), "Grandfather Spider's Feast" (Africa), "The Mirror" (Korea), "Damon & Pythias (Ancient Greece), "The Princess Who Could Not Cry" (author's original tale), "The Lion's Whisker" (Africa), "How the Mosquitos Left Kambara" (Fiji), "Clever Gretel" (Germany), "Ah Shung Catches a Ghost" (China), "Coyote Steals Spring" (Native American-Pacific Northwest), "The Chirimia" (Guatemala), "Natural Habits" (Africa), "The Magic Pot" (China), "Ada & the Rascals" (Holland), "The Miser" (United States), "The Bosung Pohoo" (India), "Little Jack & Lazy John" (France), "The Colossal Pumpkin" (Africa), "Granddaughter's Sled" (Russia), "Juan's Maguey Plant" (Mexico), "The Devil's Luck" (Hungary), "The Officer of Heaven (China), "The King Who Believed Everything" (Austria), "Hungry Spider" (Africa), "The First Lesson" (Brazil), "Peder & the Water Sprite" (Sweden), and "The Goat & the Rock" (Tibet).

The book concludes with background notes.

August House, 1993. 127 pp. Pen and ink illustrations. ISBN 0-87483-265-9

Activities

With Librarian Guidance

The troll wife is a major character in "Alexander, the Dwarf & the Troll." There are dozens of books about terrible trolls, water trolls, Christmas trolls, etc. Invite students to use the library's catalog to locate and check out one picture book about trolls. On a given day, have the students bring their books, and read their stories to the class. Then arrange a Troll Day when willing students will visit primary grade classrooms and read to a class their selected troll story.

With Classroom Teacher Guidance

1. "Granddaughter's Sled" teaches students to value senior citizens. If there is a retirement home for seniors in your community, perhaps the students could do something special for them such as make holiday table decorations, send homemade greeting cards, or present a program. If you decide on a program which might include songs and music, ask some class members to prepare stories they select from the book and present these storytellings as part of your program.

2. Tell "Ah Shung Catches a Ghost" to the class. Then have students sit in a circle. Hold a potato in your hand. Begin a ghost story. Tell a few sentences and stop at an exciting place. Pass the potato to your right. The student with the potato takes up the story, tells a few sentences, and passes the potato. When the potato gets all the way back to the teacher, end the story. (You might want to tape record this original tale as it is told.)

Tiger Soup
An Anansi Story from Jamaica
Retold and illustrated by Frances Temple

Summary

As the story begins, Tiger is down by the side of Blue Hole cooking soup. He stirs the soup with a big spoon and now and then tastes it. He has put into his sweet soup many delicious things such as coconut, mango, and nutmeg.

Anansi, the spider, comes dancing through the forest, enticed by the sweet-smelling soup. He lands right beside the tiger. Immediately Anansi begins to complain about the heat. He suggests that Tiger should swim in Blue Hole, and when Tiger explains that he doesn't swim, Anansi offers to teach him.

Anansi and Tiger go to Blue Hole and close their eyes. Anansi counts to three and throws a big coconut in the water. The Tiger jumps into Blue Hole. The Tiger finds that he likes swimming and splashes about looking for Anansi. But Anansi is on shore and quickly drinks all of Tiger's soup and scurries back to the woods. Anansi worries about what Tiger will do.

Anansi finds some little monkeys and teaches them to sing a new song. The monkeys sing, "Just a little while ago, we ate the Tiger's soup." While the monkeys are singing about the delicious soup, Tiger comes roaring out and says since they ate his soup, he will eat them. But before Tiger can catch them, the monkeys climb into the trees and swing away.

Orchard Books, 1994. 32 pp. Full-color illustrations. ISBN 0-531-08709-3

Activities

With Librarian Guidance

Anansi is a fictional spider, but real spiders are fascinating, too. Invite a class of students to work in pairs with each pair researching a different spider. Allow time for the students to tell what they learn and to show pictures of their spider. Included might be the trap-door spider, black widow, wolf spider, tarantula, crab spider, and daddy long-legs. Possible resources include magazines, encyclopedias, and nonfiction books. Students might also enjoy visiting **http://www.arizhwys.com/Wildlife/carolinawolfspider.html** and for an excellent photograph of a crab spider see **http://amwest.com/364156.htm.**

With Classroom Teacher Guidance

There are many other famous children's stories about soup. Ask interested students to find other stories in the school or public library or from home collections and to bring them to class to share and read. Among these might be: ***Dragon Soup,*** by Arlene Williams (Kramer, 1996); ***Moon Soup,*** by Lisa Desimini (Hyperion, 1993); ***Mean Soup,*** by Betsy Everitt (Harcourt Brace, 1995); ***Alphabet Soup***, by Kate Banks (Knopf, 1994); and ***Dumpling Soup*** by Jama Rattigan (Little, Brown, 1998).

With Parent/Caregiver Guidance

The author's students performed this story as a play. The playscript is on the underside of the jacket. Through your home-school newsletter, recruit a parent who would be willing to work with a group of students, using simple props and costumes, to rehearse and present this story to the class as a play.

Tongues of Jade

By Laurence Yep • Illustrated by David Wiesner

Summary

This is a collection of tales, retold from translations, passed down by Chinese Americans. The stories have been grouped into five sections.

"Roots" contains "The Green Magic, The Guardians," and "The Cure." These stories reflect the close ties that a Chinese farmer feels for the earth. Most of the Chinese who came to America in the nineteenth century provided labor for western agriculture. Many of the Chinese in America were without their families. They worked hard and, with a strong sense of responsibility, sent part of their wages home. "Family Ties" includes "The Little Emperor, Royal Robes, Fish Heads," and "The Phantom Heart." The "Wild Heart" contains "The Snake's Revenge, The Foolish Wish, Waters of Gold," and "The Tiger Cat." These stories are influenced by the effects of living in a strange land where moderation is a tactic of survival.

Shame was sometimes used to make someone conform. The three tales in the section called "Face" are "The Rat in the Wall, The Fatal Flower," and "The Teacher's Underwear."

The fact that a son was expected to honor his parents' wishes even beyond death is emphasized in the final section, "Beyond the Grave," which includes "The Magical Horse, Eyes of Jade," and "The Ghostly Rhyme."

HarperCollins, 1991. 194 pp. Black and white illustrations. ISBN 0-06-022470-3

Activities

With Librarian Guidance

In one of the stories, a monkey is mentioned. Students may wish to research and share what they learn about various monkeys and apes and related environmental groups. Begin at **http://lime.weeg.uiowa.edu/ ~ anthro/origins/primates.html.** This index will provide links to numerous topics such as the Dian Fossey Gorilla Fund, Earth Watch, chimpanzees, Golden Lion Tamarin conservation, Jane Goodall Institute, Great Ape Project, etc. Invite students to pursue one of the topics by further reading or through writing to the addresses provided.

With Classroom Teacher Guidance

In "The Fatal Flower," a young girl uses lotions to try to become more beautiful. Invite students to collect ads from newspapers and magazines for various beauty aids for men and women and bring them in to school to discuss. After studying the ads, invite students to compose a full-page magazine ad for a new grooming product. The ad may make claims for the product and may include drawings. Post these ads on a bulletin board.

With Parent/Caregiver Guidance

The librarian classroom teacher might duplicate the following letter:

Dear Parent: Your child has read Tongues of Jade *(summary attached). In "The Little Emperor," a young man learns a lesson by watching a family of birds and recognizes how he has wronged his mother. Your child might enjoy discussing with you what lessons humans might learn from observing birds, animals, fish, and insects.*

Trickster Tales
Forty Folk Stories from Around the World
Retold by Josepha Sherman • Illustrated by David Boston

Summary

This is a collection of 40 stories of tricksters from many cultures around the world including: Ancient Babylonia, Botswana, Burma, China, Egypt, French Canada, Hawaii, India, Jamaica, Japan, The Philippines, Eastern Europe, Morocco, Central and South America, as well as the Creole, African American, Algonquin, Apache, and Blackfoot peoples of North America. The trickster usually plays fairly innocent pranks and often gets away with it.

Five stories are included from Africa, seven from Europe, six from the Near East, six from Asia and Polynesia, five from Meso and South America, and six from North America. The final section on Trickster Immigrants includes one from French Canada, one from the Appalachian Mountains, one from the Southern United States, one from the Creole people of Louisiana, and one from Jamaica.

Most of the tricksters included in these stories are male. A few are human, but many of them are small and rather defenseless creatures. They depend on their wits to survive. Some of the tricksters are magical, and some can change from one form to another.

An introduction, notes, and a bibliography are included.

August House, 1996. 172 pp. Black and white illustrations. ISBN 0-87483-449-X

Activities

With Librarian Guidance

One of the stories, "The Poor Man of Nippur," comes from ancient Babylonia. Invite two students to research Babylonia and to share with the class what they learn. One place to begin is **http://www.midwinter.com/ftp/pub/TV/Babylon-5/History.Babylonia.html** which gives a short history by Shawn Bayern. Another good resource is *Sumer: Cities of Eden,* by the editors of Time Life, (Time-Life Books, 1993). Other possibilities include *Nebuchadnezzar: Scourge of Zion,* by Mark Healy (Sterling, 1989); *Babylon,* by Joan Oates (Thames & Hudson, 1986); and *Babylon: With 137 Illustrations,* by Joan Oates (Thames & Hudson, 1979).

With Classroom Teacher Guidance

1. A group of students might enjoy writing a script and acting out a sequel to "The Magic Burro." In this sequel to the original story, a trial would take place in which the "gringo" tries to get back his horse from Pedro de Urdemalas. During the trial, the trickster should again use his wits and manage to win the day. These students should write the script, rehearse, and present their play to the class.

2. There are three stories included on the theft of fire: "Fire Taking, The Theft of Fire," and "Tokwah." After students have read all three stories, hold a discussion. How are they alike? In what ways are they different? Which two of the three are most similar? Which is most interesting? Why?

The Valiant Red Rooster

By Eric A. Kimmel • Illustrated by Katya Arnold

Summary

Many versions of this folktale exist throughout Europe. This one comes from Hungary.

A rooster lives with an old woman. One morning the rooster finds the old woman weeping because there is no money and no food in the house. The rooster gathers fallen kernels of wheat, takes them to the miller to be ground into flour, then takes flour to the baker, and brings the bread home to the woman.

One day the rooster finds a diamond button. He heads for the market to buy food, but along the way a sultan spies the button and wants it. The sultan's soldiers take the button, and the rooster vows to crow at the window of the sultan's palace until the button is returned.

Each time the rooster crows at his window, the sultan tries to have the rooster killed. The rooster is thrown into a well, but he survives by drinking all the water. The rooster is put in the furnace, but puts out the fire with the water he drank. When the rooster is thrown into the beehive, he eats the bees. When the sultan puts the rooster in his trousers to sit on and crush him, the rooster lets out the bees which sting the sultan. The button is returned. The rooster exchanges it at the market for enough food to fill the old woman's house from floor to ceiling, so the old woman and rooster are never hungry again.

Henry Holt, 1995. 32 pp. Full-color illustrations. ISBN 0-8050-2781-5

Activities

With Librarian Guidance

This rooster is called a "red rooster." Students may be surprised to find out how many kinds of roosters there are. Invite a pair of students to research the varieties of chickens and to find pictures of different ones. Allow time for the students to orally share their findings with the class. An excellent site for information and pictures of American, Asiatic, English, Mediterranean, and game classes of chickens is **http://poultry.mph.msu.edu/classes.html**. Another good source of information is Gail Damerow's **Your Chickens: A Kid's Guide to Raising and Showing** (Storey Communications, 1993).

With Classroom Teacher Guidance

Real roosters have gizzards that perform a special function for the birds. Ask a pair of students to research the topic, using an encyclopedia and other available books and write a short paper, citing their sources of information. What does a gizzard do? Do any other birds besides roosters have gizzards? Post the finished paper on a bulletin board.

With Parent/Caregiver Guidance

The story of the Valiant Red Rooster might be presented as a puppet show. The teacher should recruit a parent willing to work with a group of puppeteers. Have students make puppets, which could be a combination of stick and hand puppets, rehearse with a narrator who will read the story line, and present their show to the class and perhaps another class in the school.

More Resources for Folktales From Around the World

Books

Asbjornsen, Peter Christen. *The Gruff Brothers.* Bantam, 1990.

Bernier-Grand, Carmen T. *Jean Bobo: Four Folktales from Puerto Rico.* HarperCollins, 1994.

Chang, Monica. *The Mouse Bride: A Chinese Folktale.* Pan Asian Pub., 1994.

Climo, Shirley. *Someone Saw a Spider.* Crowell, 1985.

Dee, Ruby. *Two Ways to Count to Ten: A Liberian Folktale.* Henry Holt, 1988.

Green, Robyn. *Rumpelstiltskin.* Mondo Publishing, 1995.

Hamilton, Virginia. *Her Stories: African American Folk Tales, Fairy Tales, and True Tales.* Blue Sky, 1995.

————. *The People Could Fly: American Black Folktales.* Knopf. 1985.

Harrison, Michael. *The Doom of the Gods.* Oxford University Press,1985.

Hayes, Joe. *Watch Out for Clever Women: Hispanic Folktales.* Cinco Puntas Press, 1994.

Ingpen, Robert & Barbara Hayes. *Folk Tales & Fables of the Americas & the Pacific.* Chelsea House, 1994.

————. *Folk Tales & Fables of Asia & Australia.* Chelsea House, 1994.

————. *Folk Tales & Fables of Europe.* Chelsea House, 1994.

MacDonald, Margaret Read. *Peace Tales: World Folktales to Talk About.* Linnet Books, 1992.

Martinband, Gerda. *Three Clever Mice: Folktales from Turkey, Japan, and Nepal.* Greenwillow, 1993.

Onyefulu, Obi. *Chinye: A West African Folk Tale..* Viking, 1994.

Pooley, Sarah. *Jump the World: Stories, Poems, and Things to Make and Do from Around the World.* Dutton, 1997.

Sherman, Josepha. *Trickster Tales: Forty Folk Tales from Around the World.* August House, 1996.

Tate, Eleanora E. *Don't Split the Pole: Tales of Down Home Folk Wisdom.* Delacorte Press, 1997.

Terada, Alice M. *Under the Starfruit Tree: Folktales from Vietnam.* University of Hawaii Press, 1989.

A Short Selected List of Media

Anansi. Rabbit Ears Productions.1 videocassette, 30 min. Folktales told by Denzel Washington.

The Emperor's New Clothes. Doug Molitor Home Box Office (distributed by Ambrose Video Publications), 1995. 1 videocassette and 1 study guide The classic fairy tale.

Flossie & the Fox. Patricia McKissack. Weston Woods, 1988. 1 book; 1 sound cassette, 14 min. A folktale.

The Little Samurai. Davidson, 1995. 1 computer laser optical disc. Requires Mac LC575 or IBM Windows 95. A Japanese folk tale.

The Princess and the Pea. Susan Kim. Home Box Office, (distributed by Ambrose Video Publishing), 1995. 1 videocassette with study guide. A well-known fairy tale.

Puss in Boots. Hanna-Barbera Home Video, 1991. 1 videocassette, 30 min. An animated adaptation of Charles Perrault's classic folktale.

The Rainbow People. Laurence Yep. Recorded Books, 1993. 3 sound cassettes, 240 min. A telling of twenty Chinese folk tales.

The Steadfast Tin Soldier. Hanna Barbera Home Video, 1991. 1 videocassette, 30 min. An adaptation of Hans Christian Andersen's classic tale.

A Story, A Story. Gail E. Haley. Weston Woods, 1993. 1 book; 1 sound cassette, 22 min. African folktales.

The Tiger and the Brahmin. Rabbit Ears Productions, distributed by UNI Distribution Corp., 1991. 1 videocassette, 30 min. Traditional Indian folktales.

American Tall Tales

By Mary Pope Osborne • Illustrated by Michael McCurdy

Summary

This collection of retellings of tall tales presents a picture of nineteenth-century America. The tales include a range of geographic settings and illustrate the different occupations which contributed to the development of our country including backwoodsmen and women, sea captains, volunteer firefighters, farmers, cowboys and cowgirls, railroad workers, and loggers.

Some of the central characters such as Davy Crockett and Johnny Appleseed were actual people who lived during the first half of the 1800s. As stories about these men were told, events in their lives became exaggerated and they became folk heroes. Other characters such as Pecos Bill and Febold Feboldson were inventions of professional newspaper and magazine writers. Sally Ann Thunder Ann Whirlwind Crockett was introduced in one of the *Davy Crockett Almanacks*.

In addition to the nine stories which are included, there is a map of the United States indicating where Davy Crockett, Sally Ann Thunder Ann Whirlwind, Johnny Appleseed, Stormalong, Mose, Febold Feboldson, Pecos Bill, John Henry and Paul Bunyan performed the feats that gave them heroic status. The book also includes a bibliography.

Knopf, 1991. 116 pp. Illustrated with color wood engravings. ISBN 0-679-80089-1

Activities

With Librarian Guidance

Davy Crockett died at the Alamo in 1836. Invite a small group of students to research this topic. Where is the Alamo and why was a battle fought there? What did each side hope to gain? Who were the leaders on each side? Ask these students to write a short report, with a bibliography, sharing what they learn. Information about the battle site and history can be found at **http://www.imax.sa.com/alamo.htm.** Two useful books are ***Davy Crockett: Defender of the Alamo***, by William R. Sanford (Enslow, 1996) and ***The Alamo,*** by William W. Lace (Lucent Books, 1998).

With Classroom Teacher Guidance

1. The life of Johnny Appleseed (John Chapman) is an interesting one. Have a group of students research and give an oral report on this man. Useful information can be found at **http://www.appleseed.org/johnny.html** and in ***John Chapman: The Man Who Was Johnny Appleseed*** by Carol Greene (Children's Press, 1991) and ***Johnny Appleseed*** by Gini Holland (Raintree Steck Vaughn, 1997).

2. "Mose" tells about a time when volunteer firemen in New York pulled "pumpers" through the streets of the city. Today's fire trucks are very different. Ask if a local fire station can send a truck to school with fire fighters who can explain how the truck works. Follow up the visit with thank you notes to the firemen who shared their time and expertise.

Big Men, Big Country
A Collection of American Tall Tales
By Paul Robert Walker • Illustrated by James Bernardin

Summary

This is a collection of nine fantastic tales. Each is followed with information detailing its origin.

The first story, "Davy Crockett Teaches the Steamboat a Leetle Patriotism," describes what happens when Davy tries to take his bear, Death Hug, with him on a steamboat ride. "Old Stormalong Finds a Man-Sized Ship" tells how a huge sailor finally finds a ship big enough to suit him and explains how the White Cliffs of Dover and the Panama Canal came to be. In "Big Mose and the Lady Washington," there is a daring rescue of three children from the fifth floor of a burning building.

In "John Darling and the Skeeter Chariot," giant mosquitoes carry John Darling from California to China and then back home to the Catskill Mountains. The laws of gravity are defied in "Ol' Gabe in the Valley of the Yellowstone." One of the most famous of the Bunyan stories is related in "Paul Bunyan and the Winter of the Blue Snow." In "John Henry Races the Steam Drill," the steel-driving man dies after beating the drill. It takes a boa constrictor and a needle and thread to strike oil in "Gib Morgan Brings in the Well." Pecos Bill makes a big mistake when he allows his bride to ride his horse, Widow Maker, in "Pecos Bill Finds a Ranch But Loses a Wife."

Harcourt Brace Jovanovich, 1993. 79 pp. Full-color illustrations. ISBN 0-15-207136-9

Activities

With Librarian Guidance

Ol' Gabe is another name for Jim Bridger, a famous mountain man. Ask students to research Jim Bridger. When and where did he live? For what activities did he become famous? Have these students write a report on Jim Bridger including a bibliography that lists at least three sources of information. Resources include: **http://www.isu.edu/~trinmich/Ft.Bridger.htm.** for information about the fort and direct quotes from Bridger and others. Also see *Jim Bridger: The Mountain Man,* by Dan Zadra, (Creative Education, 1988) and *Trappers & Traders,* by Gail Stewart (Rourke, 1990).

With Classroom Teacher Guidance

1. Part of the charm of Davy Crockett's story comes from some of the made-up words that are used: "splendiferous rifle, humanish critter, felt totalaciously better." Ask students to write an original anecdote about any one of the figures in this book and include a few "original" words in the story. Allow time for those who wish to share these tall tales aloud.

2. Old Stormalong explains how the Courser cut through the Isthmus of Panama. Actually making the Panama Canal was a little more complicated. Invite a pair of students to research this topic and orally share what they learn. See Tim McNeese's book, *The Panama Canal,* (Lucent Books, 1997) and visit **http:www.pananet.com/pancanal/public/public.htm** for photographs and information on the history and operations of the canal.

 *Tall Tales: 3*

Cannonball River Tales

By David Rounds • Illustrated by Alix Berenzy

Summary

The book is divided into five chapters, each describing the adventures of Tom Terry, whose home is the farmland by the banks of the magical Cannonball River. The stories are a blend of foolishness, fantasy, and a love of nature.

The first chapter is called "Tom Builds a Fort That Isn't Entirely." Using the roof that blew off of Farmer Feboldsson's barn in a tornado, Tom builds a fort. He doesn't have enough lumber to finish it, but a grain spirit named Wheatberry appears and lends a hand.

In the second chapter, "Tom Changes His Eating Habits," Tom meets a rabbit that is a tree spirit, and decides to quit hunting. In "Tom Keeps a Promise," Tom's boasting catches up with him. He is shamed into clearing a dam from the Water Spirit's river but uses up all his extra strength in one night.

Tom was jealous of his wife's cousin Febold. But in trying to better his cousin, Tom stirs up a dragon in "Tom Digs for Silver." Tom is old and building a retirement home in "Tom Goes to the Bearback Races." His grandson, Nick, joins him in talking with the forestmen, bear, and Jack Pine. As a result of the talk, they move the site of the retirement house.

Sierra Club Books for Children, 1992. 97 pp. Decorative illustrations. ISBN 0-87156-577-3

Activities

With Librarian Guidance

Tom's valley suffered a drought. Have two students find out what the average rainfall is in your town or city by using the archives of your local newspaper. (Sometimes the index to the local newspaper is available on the Internet. If not, the students should call the local paper, and be referred to the correct editor to seek out this information.) The students should find out: What was the driest year to date? What was the wettest year on record? What is the average rainfall? Is this current year an "average" year? Ask the students to share what they learn in an oral report.

With Classroom Teacher Guidance

With help from the art educator, a group of students might enjoy making a large mural depicting the *Cannonball River Tales*. This mural could be divided into five sections showing the major events from Tom's youth to his old age. Students could use collage techniques and/or tempera paint. Display the completed mural on a large wall.

With Parent/Caregiver Guidance

The librarian or classroom teacher might duplicate and send home the following letter.

Dear Parent: Your child has read Cannonball River Tales *(summary attached). If Tom Terry actually lived today in our country, he might be called an environmentalist. Your child might enjoy discussing with you what an environmentalist is and what environmental issues have recently been in the news either locally or nationally.*

 *Tall Tales:* 4

Chuck Wagon Stew

Written and illustrated by E.J. Bird

Summary

These nine tall tales are all set in the West. In the first story, "Blood Brothers," Swen and Olaf send one another packages filled with strange creatures certain to pester one another. "Old Three Toes" tells the story of a legendary bear and its raids on local farms. "Big Red and the Jay Bird" depicts the unusual friendship between two animals that continues even after one of them dies.

In "The Outlaws," when one of three bank robbers gets killed, the other two return to the doctor that treated him. They are very interested in the coat the dead man was wearing.

"Big Money" tells of an outlaw's wise decision to cut loose the money he's robbed from a bank and save his horse in the river. "Miss Lily" shows that women as well as men can ride and shoot and survive in the West. "Huckleberries for Breakfast" describes a very unusual way of milking a cow.

The old cowhands in "Gone to Fetch the Bull" are worried when a young city kid fails to turn up at the ranch with the bull. They are even more surprised to find out how the boy finally got back to the ranch. "Owl Feather" tells the story of an old Shoshone Indian and how he survives a long cold winter when he learns it isn't his time to die.

Carolrhoda Books, 1988. 72 pp. Color pen and ink illustrations. ISBN 0-87614-313-3

Activities

With Librarian Guidance

The author of this book has done his own illustrations. One of the most famous illustrators of the American West was Frederic Remington. Invite a pair of students to research this topic, write a short report, and find pictures of some of his work to share with the class. Resources include: *Frederic Remington,* by Elizabeth Van Steinwyk (Franklin Watts, 1994) and *Remington & Russell: The Sid Richardson Collection,* by Brian W. Dippie (Univ. of Texas Press, 1994). If you have access to them, share with students the *Oxford Companion to Art* (Oxford University Press, 1970) and *Encyclopedia of World Art* (Heraty, 1983).

With Classroom Teacher Guidance

1. One of the characters mentioned in the book is Smokey, a Shoshone Indian. Ask a pair of students to find out where the Shoshone Indians once lived. What sort of homes did they have? How did they live? Who were their enemies? Using a map of the U.S., ask these students to share their information with the class in an oral report. A good resource is *The Shoshone Indians* by Nathaniel Moss (Chelsea Juniors, 1997).

2. On page 39, the reader is asked how much $20,000 weighs. In the late 1800s, how much did a $100 gold piece weigh? How much would 200 such gold pieces weigh? How much does today's silver dollar weigh? How much would 20,000 silver dollars weigh? To find the answers to these questions, students might begin with a local coin shop, or try **www.money.org/ynschapp.html** which is the Web site for the Education Department of the American Numismatic Association. Have these students share what they learn.

Cut From the Same Cloth
American Women of Myth, Legend, and Tall Tale
By Robert D. San Souci • Illustrated by Brian Pinkney

Summary

This collection contains stories about legendary American women, drawn from folktales, popular stories, and ballads. The stories are collected from five geographic regions and represent Anglo American, African American, Spanish American, and various Native American tribes.

Included in the section on "Women of the Northeast" are "The Star Maiden, Bess Call," and "Drop Star." Representatives of the "Women of the South" are "Molly Cottontail, Annie Christmas," and "Susanna and Simon." The stories selected from "Women of the Midwest" are "Sal Fink, Sweet Betsey from Pike," and "Old Sally Cato." Included in the stories of "Women of the Southwest" are "Pale-Faced Lightning, Pohaha," and "Sister Fox and Brother Coyote." The section, "Women of the West," includes "Hekeke, Otoonah," and "Hiiaka."

The stories deal with many topics: women who control the power of fire and lightning; women who were giant-slayers; women strong enough to triumph over the heat and thirst of desert or the cold and near starvation conditions of an arctic winter; and female animals like Sister Fox who is a trickster and proves as resourceful as Brother Coyote or of Molly Cottontail who is the counterpart of Br'er Rabbit.

Philomel, 1993. 149 pp. Black and white illustrations. ISBN 0-399-21987-0

Activities

With Librarian Guidance

The story, "Pale-Faced Lightning," is set in a region near Phoenix called Mount Superstition where there are eroded rock formations that resemble figures. Ask two students, with the help of Uncover, or the *Reader's Guide* to locate issues of magazines containing photographs of some of the strange rock formations in Arizona. Try to borrow copies of appropriate magazines (such as *Arizona Highways)* and bring them to share with class members. Information and a good picture can be found at **http://www.public.asu.ed/ ~ gtb8923/azindex.html.**

With Classroom Teacher Guidance

1. A map is found at the beginning of the book. Invite a pair of students to make their own colorful map to hang on a bulletin board in the library. The students should make and label symbols for the legendary women discussed in the book and place these symbols in the right places on the map.

2. "Annie Christmas" runs a flat-bottomed boat up and down the Mississippi River. Ask two students to research river traffic on the Mississippi. What goods were carried on these boats? What happened when the boats reached New Orleans? How did the river traffic change over the years? Have these students write a short paper, including a bibliography, and post it on a bulletin board or school Web site. Two good references are *The Mississippi,* by Michael Pollard (Benchmark, 1997) and *The Mississippi,* by Nina Morgan (Raintree Steck-Vaughn, 1994).

Fin M'Coul
The Giant of Knockmany Hill
Retold and illustrated by Tomie dePaola

Summary

This is a story about the popular Irish giant, Fin M'Coul, and another giant named Cucullin, who has a reputation for being the strongest giant in Ireland. The earth quakes when he walks. All the other giants, including Fin M'Coul, are afraid of him. Cucullin carries in his pocket a flattened thunderbolt.

Although Cucullin has given most of the giants a good beating, he has never been able to catch up with Fin M'Coul. When Fin learns that Cucullin is in his neighborhood, he runs to his home on Knockmany Hill and to his wife, Oonagh.

Oonagh encourages her husband not to run away again. She works a charm and is confident she can protect him. She bakes loaves of bread with iron frying pans hidden in them. She puts white stones alongside pieces of pale cheese. Then she hides her husband, dressed as a baby, in a cradle.

When Cucullin arrives, Oonagh invites him in. She gives him bread, and he breaks his teeth. He breaks more teeth when he tries to eat stones which he thinks are cheese. When Cucullin checks Baby-Fin's teeth, Fin M'Coul bites off his brass finger which is the source of Cucullin's strength and then beats him up. Cucullin runs away and never bothers Fin M'Coul again.

Holiday House, 1981. 32 pp. Color illustrations. ISBN 0-8234-0384-X

Activities

With Librarian Guidance

Baby-Fin squeezes water out of cheese. A small group of students might want to research cheese making and share what they learn in an oral report to the class. They may wish to read *Cheese,* by Linda Illsley (Carolrhoda, 1991) and *Milk*, by Dorothy Turner (Carolrhoda, 1989). Students can follow the six steps of cheese making at **http://web.tusco.net/broadrun/cheesemak.htm** or visit a farm where gouda cheese is made at **http://www.winchestercheese.com/index.html.**

With Classroom Teacher Guidance

Fin M'Coul is working on a giant's highway to connect Ireland with Scotland. Ask a pair of students to use an atlas with a scale of miles to find the two countries. At the closest point, how far apart are they? If one goes by boat, what are the major port cities? Ask the students to share what they learn. Students may wish to read *Ireland*, by Patricia Marjorie Levy (Marshall Cavendish, 1994) and *Scotland,* by Doreen Taylor (Raintree Steck Vaughn, 1991).

Cucullin carries a "thunderbolt" in his pocket. Invite a group of students to research thunder and lightning. What conditions must be present for such a storm to occur? What causes the noise and the flash through the sky? The students should write a brief paper of explanation. They might consult *Weather,* by Sally Morgan (Time-Life, 1996) or *Lightning*, by Seymour Simon (Morrow, 1997).

 *Tall Tales: 7*

The Hair of the Bear
Campfire Yarns and Short Stories
By Eric A. Bye • Illustrated by Tom Elisii

Summary

This book contains twenty-three tall tales. The appeal of these stories lies partly in their humor and partly in their reflection of the adventurous lifestyle of the early American frontier.

The stories have diverse origins. Some are original and some share the language of frontier writers and personal narratives of trappers and explorers. Some are written in correct English and others are in the colorful language associated with pioneers. It is recommended that the first story, "Semi-Glossary," be read before the others since, in the context of the story, there are explanations of many terms and expressions which appear throughout the book.

The stories included are: "Semi-Glossary, Checkmate, My Disagreement With a Sarpent, A Strong Attraction, Outfoxed, Fresh Bait, Uncle Eef's Rifle, How I Acted in My Own Defense, A Narrow Escape, Freezin' Tunes, A Favor Repaid, A Rancantankerous Rifle Barrel, Ol' Broken Wind, Delivered from the Spirit Trail, The Great Buffler Chase, How I Saved My Life by Shooting Myself, The Catamount and the Big Swallow, A Partnership, Prospecting On the Winneanimus, A Pilgrim's Progress, Bat Eye's Last Laugh, The Track of the Windigo," and "Pickbone's Victory Dash."

Eagle's View Publishing, 1991. 182 pp. Black and white illustrations. ISBN 0-943604-30-3

Activities

With Librarian Guidance

"Semi-Glossary" explains a lot of vocabulary. Ask students to choose a familiar topic that they enjoy and know a lot about (sailing, soccer, cooking, etc.) and write a short essay or story using specialized words which they explain during their writing. Students should be encouraged to check out books on their topic of interest and check each book's glossary of terms for ideas on what to include and how to briefly explain the specialized vocabulary.

With Classroom Teacher Guidance

In the story, "Freezing Times," the author reports "snow was turning blue from the cold." Ask a pair of students to research snow-related topics such as crystals and avalanches. Students might visit Snow on the Web at **http://eosins.colorado.edu/NSIDC/EDUCATION/SNOW/web_resources.html.** Information on electron microscopy at **http://www.ioppublishing.com/IOP/Groups/EM/** is a good site for more advanced students. Allow time for students to share what they learn.

With Parent/Caregiver Guidance

The librarian or classroom teacher might duplicate the following:

Dear Parent: Your child has read "How I Acted in My Own Defense" from The Hair of the Bear *(summary attached) and has the assignment of writing a letter home describing a stagecoach attack. Would you review your child's rough draft and offer suggestions that will make the letter lively and descriptive?*

Larger Than Life
The Adventures of American Legendary Heroes
By Robert D. San Souci • Illustrated by Andrew Glass

Summary

The first story in the collection is "John Henry: The Steel-Driving Man." John Henry, a big and powerful young man, pits his strength and skill as a steel driver for the railroad against a machine in order to save the jobs of the men. John Henry wins, but in driving himself so hard, he dies.

"Old Stormalong: The Deep-Water Sailor" follows the escapades of a giant sailor as he moves from ship to ship and from one adventure to another, always seeking a bigger and bigger ship on which to sail the sea.

In "Slue-Foot Sue and Pecos Bill," two legendary figures meet and fall in love. Their wedding day turns into such a disaster that the bride leaves. But finally coming to her senses, she returns to find Pecos Bill.

In "Strap Buckner: The Texas Fighter," Strap becomes famous for fighting anyone and anything. He takes on a huge, black bull named Noche, two Indian traders, an Indian chief and his tribe, and finally meets his match when he fights the devil.

"Paul Bunyan and Babe the Blue Ox," is one version of the story of how Paul finds and raises Babe. The book also offers stories about their prowess and their joyful life together after they finally retire.

Doubleday, 1991. 59 pp. Full-color illustrations. ISBN 0-385-24907-1

Activities

With Librarian Guidance

Students may be interested in learning more about octopuses, which appear in one of the stories. Ask a small group to carry out research and report to the class what they learn. Useful books include: **Octopus,** by Rebecca Stefoff (Benchmark Books, 1997) and **Octopuses: Underwater Jet Propulsion,** by Andreu Llamas (Gareth Stevens, 1996). Two good spots on the Net for pictures and an introduction to Cephalopods are: **http://is.dal.ca/~ceph/wood.htm** and **http://www.marinelab.sarasota.fl.us/OCTOPI.htm.**

With Classroom Teacher Guidance

In the story "Old Stormalong: The Deep Water Sailor," Stormalong ties the arms of an octopus in eight knots: reef knot, half hitch, bowline, sheepshank, stunner hitch, cat's paw, becket bend, and fisherman's bend. Invite to class someone who can tie and show these different knots to the students. Be sure the visit is followed up with a student-written thank you note.

With Parent/Caregiver Guidance

The librarian or classroom teacher might duplicate the following letter:

Dear Parent: Your child has read Larger Than Life *(summary attached). In these tall tales, Paul Bunyan and his ox are attributed with creating U.S. geography. Paul dug the Great Lakes to give his ox fresh water. Your child is to write an original adventure for Paul and Babe in which some geographic feature is created by them. It would be helpful if you would discuss this assignment with your child and provide suggestions and input.*

Mike Fink

Retold and illustrated by Steven Kellogg

Summary

The story of Mike Fink begins when he is only two days old and runs away from home because he hates being shut up indoors. His grandfather goes out with a net and catches Mike, determined that the boy will behave like a normal infant.

But back home again, Mike still hates being indoors. He jumps up and down on his bed and catapults right through the roof. While flying through the air, Mike spies keelboats. When he bounces back down, he announces he wants to be a keelboatman. His mother decides to raise him on the frontier.

Mike loves the frontier, but he hasn't forgotten keelboats. His skill with a rifle lands him a job as a scout. He meets up with Jack Carpenter, King of the Keelboatmen, who wrestles with him and throws Mike into the Rocky Mountains. There, Mike practices with wrestling bears. He goes back, beats Jack Carpenter, and is made captain of a keelboat. Mike proves his skills in his work and in races and games. He earns the name King of the Keelboatmen.

When steamboats begin competing with keelboats, Mike Fink challenges Skipper Hilton Blathersby. The keelboat is sunk, and the steamboat blows up, but Blathersby and Fink survive. They wrestle, and some say Blathersby was thrown to grizzly-bear country. Mike Fink remains King of the Keelboatmen.

Morrow Junior Books, 1992. 40 pp. Full-color illustrations. ISBN 0-688-07004-3

Activities

With Librarian Guidance

Mike Fink hates steamboats. Ask two students to write a short research paper about the history of steamboats. They should list three sources of information. They might want to consult ***Robert Fulton,*** by Elaine Landau (Franklin Watts, 1991); ***A Head Full of Notions: A Story About Robert Fulton***, by Andy Russell Bowen (Carolrhoda, 1997) and ***The Marshall Cavendish Illustrated Guide to Steamships,*** by Christopher Chant (Marshall Cavendish, 1989). A useful Web site is **http://www.history.rochester.edu/steam/brown/chpt4.html.**

With Classroom Teacher Guidance

1. Mike Fink's grandparents were opposed both to keelboatmen and to life on the frontier. Suggest that students pretend to be Mike Fink and write a letter to his grandparents. He should tell his relatives back home all about his life on the river. (Remember that this letter can be a tall tale, too, filled with imaginary adventures!) Post the letters on a bulletin board.

2. Often a hero is used on television to promote a product. A movie star may promote a line of jewelry, perfume, or clothing. A sports star may promote athletic shoes. Discuss with the class some of the ads they have seen. Then have students write a 60-second television commercial in which Mike Fink is used to promote a product. What product will be promoted? Will there be a slogan? Invite students to read to the class in their best broadcasting voices the commercials they write.

A Million Fish... More Or Less

By Patricia C. McKissack • Illustrated by Dena Schutzer

Summary

This story takes place on the Bayou Clapateaux in Louisiana.

Hugh Thomas is fishing from the bank when Papa-Daddy and Elder Abbajon come rowing out of the river fog and immediately begin telling stories. Papa-Daddy says in 1903, he and the Elder caught a 500-pound turkey. Elder Abbajon takes up the story and explains that while they were carrying the turkey home, they found a lantern left by the Spanish conquistadors in 1542, and it was still burning.

Papa-Daddy adds that the turkey got away when they were chased by a snake with arms and legs. And Elder Abbajon explains that mosquitoes caused him to drop the lantern in quicksand.

Hugh Thomas smiles and says that they are "just funning," and the two men row away. Hugh Thomas catches more than a million fish which he packs onto his wagon. A huge alligator blocks his way and demands half the fish. With the other half of his fish, he heads for the houseboat but finds himself surrounded by an army of raccoons. Hugh Thomas challenges the head of the band to a jump rope contest and wins, so the raccoons take only half the fish. Flocks of birds take some of the fish, cats take more, and Hugh Thomas has only three fish to take to Papa-Daddy and Elder Abbajon. But he also brings them a story.

Knopf, 1992. 32 pp. Full-color illustrations. ISBN 0-679-80692-X

Activities

With Librarian Guidance

Invite a small group of students to study alligators and crocodiles and share what they learn with the class. Resources include: ***The American Alligator,*** by Steve Potts (Capstone, 1998), ***Alligators & Crocodiles,*** by Karen Dudley (Raintree Steck Vaughn, 1998) and ***The Crocodiles*** by Phyllis J. Perry (Franklin Watts, 1997). Learn about reproduction, feeding, and habitats at **http://gnv.ifas.ufl.edu/www/agator/htm/aligator.htm** or **http://www.fws.gov/ ~ r9extaff/bio-logues/bio_alli.htm.**

With Classroom Teacher Guidance

Ask a pair of students to research Louisiana. Have four students present a panel discussion telling about its geography, history, people, and customs. Sources of information include **http://www.sec.state.la.us/brief-/.htm** and ***Louisiana,*** by Capstone Press Geography Dept., (Capstone Press, 1996) and ***Louisiana,*** by Suzanne LeVert (Benchmark Books, 1997).

With Parent/Caregiver Guidance

The teacher might send home the following letter.

Dear Parent: Our math puzzle problem this week is based on a tall tale that the students have read. Please discuss this problem with your child and offer suggestions as to the ways your child might solve it. Your child should bring his/her solution to school by this Friday when we'll discuss the problem in class. Problem: If an alligator moves at one hundred yards per second, about how many minutes would it take to go a mile?

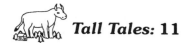

Papa Alonzo Leatherby
A Collection of Tall Tales from the Best Storyteller in Carroll County
by Marguerite W. Davol

Summary

The story is set in Carroll County many years ago when there were no automobiles or airplanes. Papa Alonzo, his wife, and their nine children live in a little house in the woods. Often in the evening, Papa Alonzo tells his family stories.

The book is divided into nine chapters. The first chapter, "The Coldest Night of the Year," tells about a night that was so cold, Papa Alonzo's words froze as they came out of his mouth. In "The Mammoth Maple," Papa Alonzo finds a single tree that gives so much syrup he loses his fondness for it.

"The Gravel-Voiced Bear" spoils Papa Alonzo's tea party and scares a neighbor half to death. "Willy's Ravenous Raccoons" explains why the raccoons didn't eat the farm crops but came right to the house to eat from the puppy's dish.

"Summer Soup" describes a season that is so hot the apples in the orchard stewed themselves into apple sauce. "The Day the Goat Turned Blue" describes all the fun and tribulations of going to a fair. "Put Her in a Pumpkin Shell" tells what happens when one of the children falls inside a giant pumpkin. "Talking Turkey" explains why a turkey was missing from the Thanksgiving feast. And "The Tallest Christmas Tree in Carroll County" tells about decorating a love-sick moose.

Simon & Schuster, 1995. 70pp. No illustrations. ISBN 0-689-80278-1

Activities

With Librarian Guidance

Ask a small group of students to research maple syrup. How is maple syrup tapped? What process does it go through before it reaches your table? Ask these students to make a large wall chart with pictures and captions explaining the steps that are used in making maple syrup. A good site is **http://www.spruceharbor.com/commun ~ 1/kitchen/maple.htm** and more pictures are available at **http://www.goshen.edu/ ~ larryry/photos.htm.** Useful print resources include **Sugaring Season: Making Maple Syrup,** by Diane Burns (Carolrhoda Books, 1990) and **Vermont,** by Dan Elish (Benchmark Books, 1997).

With Classroom Teacher Guidance

1. The pumpkin grown on the Leatherby farm was big. Introduce your students to whatever books your library has to locate information on world records. (*The Guinness Book of World Records* might be one.) Consult available sources to learn about the weight of the heaviest pumpkin ever grown. How big was it and where was it raised? Students might want to encourage class members to guess before reporting their information.

2. A group of students might want to check on cold weather temperatures in your town. (The local newspaper archives may be a good source of information.) When was the coldest night last year and how cold did it get? What is the record for the coldest night in your town? Have these students report their information to the class and tell how they found their information.

Sally Ann Thunder Ann Whirlwind Crockett

Retold and illustrated by Steven Kellogg

Summary

The author explains that many of America's tall tales have roots in the Davy Crockett almanacs which were published from 1834 to 1856. This picturebook version draws from a number of these almanac tales about Davy Crockett's wife.

Sally Ann was born in Kentucky, the first girl in a family with nine boys. She immediately races her brothers to the top of the mountain and wins. Throughout her youth, Sally Ann astonishes people by winning races, flipping arm wrestlers, and by being a champion on the tug-of-war team.

On her eighth birthday, Sally Ann leaves for the frontier. She lives with animals and learns their habits. When it gets cold, she snuggles next to a bear in a cave. The bear awakes, but Sally Ann's smile causes him to fall over backwards and be skinned by the sharp stalactites and stalagmites.

Sally Ann wraps up in the bearskin and heads for new adventures. When she grows up, she comes upon Davy Crockett and rescues him, inventing bald eagles at the same time. They marry and start a family. While her husband is away, Sally fights off alligators by kicking up a tornado. When Mike Fink tries to trick her, Sally Ann throws him five miles up river.

Morrow Junior Books, 1995. 42 pp. Full-color illustrations. ISBN 0-688-14043-2

Activities

With Librarian Guidance

Sally Ann offers an imaginative explanation of bald eagles. A group of students may wish to learn some facts about these birds and how they are used as a symbol for our country. Sources of information include: ***The Bald Eagle,*** by Steve Potts (Capstone Press, 1998), ***Bald Eagles,*** by James E. Gerholdt (Abdo & Daughters, 1997), and for a discussion of the eagle as a symbol ***The American Eagle,*** by Lynda Sorensen (Rourke, 1994). Students should report orally to the class what they learn.

With Classroom Teacher Guidance

1. The alligator on top of Sally Ann's roof is one of several kinds of animals called "crocodilians." Invite a group of students to identify other crocodilians, drawing a picture of each, accompanied by facts about size and habitat. One good resource is ***The Crocodilians: Reminders of the Days of Dinosaurs,*** by Phyllis J. Perry (Franklin Watts: 1997). Have the students post their reports and drawings on a bulletin board or on a school Web site.

2. Sally Ann can stay underwater for over an hour. Students may wonder how fish can breathe under water. Have them research and then explain to the class how fish breathe, using a diagram that they have prepared. Clear data for this project can be found by clicking on gills at **http://vif199.icair.iac.org.nz/education/resource/selfstud/fishst/nature.htm**. Another resource is ***What Is a Fish?*** by Robert Snedden (Sierra Club Books, 1993).

Some of the Adventures of Rhode Island Red

By Stephen Manes • Illustrated by William Joyce

Summary

This book contains an introduction and seven chapters. An old farmer tells the story of the greatest hero who ever lived, Rhode Island Red. A writer, who hears the story, records it.

In chapter one, Rhode Island Red is discovered in Mrs. Huckaby's henhouse in a nest. He is a baby boy no bigger than a toenail. Old Rhody, the hen, raises him. Finding himself a failure at school, Red goes off to seek fame and fortune. In chapters two and three, Red meets up with some skinny chickens and convinces the farmer to take better care of them. He protects the chickens from foxes and other dangers.

In chapters four and five, Red sets out again to seek his fortune and takes with him one of the chickens, Big Tom. They meet up with Julius and Elsinore, out-of-work servants, and walk together to Providence. In Providence, Red is re-united with his rich father, learns how he was lost as a child, and secures employment for his friends.

In chapter six, Red tries to win the mayor's daughter for his wife, by fulfilling campaign promises and getting the mayor re-elected. Rejected, Red sets off for home. And in chapter seven, the writer may or may not, meet Rhode Island Red.

J.B. Lippincott, 1990. 117 pp. Black and white illustrations. ISBN 0-397-32348-4

Activities

With Librarian Guidance

Rhode Island Red can speak chicken and human. Humans have tried to communicate with chimpanzees and with dolphin. Have a group of interested students use the *Reader's Guide to Periodical Literature* or a computerized periodical index to find articles about inter-species communication. Ask the students, with permission, to make a copy of any of the articles that they find and to share these with the class.

With Classroom Teacher Guidance

Rhode Island is a small state. Ask a group of students to prepare a written report about this state, including a bibliography of at least three sources of information. In their report, they should answer these questions: When did Rhode Island become a state? How big is it? What are its main products and industries? Possible resources include **Rhode Island**, by Kathleen Thompson (Raintree Steck-Vaughn, 1996), J.F. Warner's **Rhode Island** (Lerner, 1993.), and the Web site **http://www.relin.state.ri.us/studteaguide/RhodeIslandHistory/rodehist.html**.

With Parent/Caregiver Guidance

The classroom teacher or librarian might send home the following letter.

Dear Parent: Your child has read Some of the Adventures of Rhode Island Red *(summary attached). In most tall tales, the hero is big, but Rhode Island Red is no bigger than an egg. Your child might enjoy discussing with you how the author tries to make such a small character a hero. Does the author succeed? Why?*

A Tall Story and Other Tales

By Margaret Mahy • Illustrated by Jan Nesbitt

Summary

This book contains eleven stories. The first, "A Tall Story," is a typical tall tale. Uncle Ted exaggerates more and more as he tells a doubting niece how he went hunting for a giant land-dwelling oyster that was as big as a town hall.

The ten stories that follow have elements of realism, exaggeration, and fantasy. In "Aunt Nasty" the family worries about Aunt Nasty's visit because she is a witch. In "Kite Saturday," Joan's wish comes true when she gives an old woman her silver coin. Many odd coincidences occur in "Telephone Detectives" in which a buried treasure is found. Mrs. Bartelmy is a pirate with a wooden leg. In "Mrs. Bartelmy's Pet," she chooses a lion rather than a cat for a companion. A broomstick-riding, fiddle-playing dog rides with Mrs. Rose because she has an allergy to cats.

"The Breakfast Bird" explains how a boy adds a budgie to his family. In "Teddy and the Witches," Teddy makes the witches reverse their spells. In "The Boy Who Went Looking for a Friend," Sam finds a tiger, monkeys, and a circus but settles for a boy named Philip for his friend. In "Patrick Comes to School," Patrick turns out to be a riddle to the other children. Sammy doesn't realize he's found a ghost in "Looking for a Ghost."

M. K. McElderry, 1992. 88 pp. Black and white and full-color illustrations. ISBN 0-689-50547-7

Activities

With Librarian Guidance

Learning to use human resources when researching the answer to questions is an important skill. In the story, Patrick has red hair and freckles. Who in your community might be able to explain: What makes red hair red? And is there a reason that some red-headed people have lots of freckles? Brainstorm ideas. Have the students compose a letter inviting a knowledgeable and appropriate person to visit the class and answer these questions.

With Classroom Teacher Guidance

Class members sit in a circle, each holding onto a long circular string, on which a button has been threaded. The teacher begins the tall tale by naming the setting and characters. "Two teenagers, Bob and Betty, found themselves alone in a deep, dark forest. They heard a weird sound in the bushes, and out jumped ..." The teacher passes the button to her left and that student adds a few sentences before passing the button on. Make each addition fantastic. Tape record the session to replay later.

With Art Educator Guidance

Plan a kite afternoon. The art educator can help students make kites using balsa wood sticks and tissue paper. Interested students should bring in balls of twine and may try to fly kites in a wire-free area on the school grounds or a in near-by park on a windy day. The classroom teacher might follow up by having the students write kite poems which could be mounted around a student-made kite and make an attractive bulletin board.

Tall, Wide, and Sharp-Eye

Retold and illustrated by Mirko Gabler

Summary

As this Czech tale opens, the king gives his son a key to a room at the top of the tower and tells him he will find his future queen there. The prince looks at pictures of princesses hung there. One of the pictures is covered with a curtain. He draws the curtain, sees a princess, and decides she's the one for him.

The prince sets off to find his princess who is kept under lock and key in an evil sorcerer's castle. He gets lost in the forest and hears people calling him. They are Tall One, Wide One, and Sharp-Eye. The prince decides to take them along with him.

They come to the dark castle and go to the dining room where there is light and food. While they are eating, a sorcerer appears and explains that the prince must successfully guard the princess for three nights if he wants to marry her.

Next morning, the princess is gone. Sharp-Eye sees her in an acorn in the wood, and Tall One quickly brings her back. The second morning, Sharp-Eye sees the princess hidden in a diamond in the mountains. Tall One brings her back. The third morning, Sharp-Eye sees the princess in a shell in the sea. Wide One drinks some sea water so Tall One can pick up the shell and throw it back to the castle just in time. The sorcerer turns into a raven and flies away. Everyone in the castle wakes again.

Henry Holt, 1994. 32 pp. Color illustrations. ISBN 0-8050-2784-X

Activities

With Librarian Guidance

1. In this story, the sorcerer casts a spell so that the princess becomes a pearl in a shell. Ask a small group of students to research pearls and orally share what they learn. What causes a pearl to grow? Do pearls come in different colors? Possible sources of information include: ***Underwater Animals: Over 300 Fun Facts for Curious Kids***, by Annabell Donati (Golden Books, 1994). Find excellent pictures of different varieties of pearls at **http://www.dillonpearl.com/variety.html** and data on how a pearl is born is at **http://www.chandranipearls.com/diff.html.**

2. There are different books that list world records. Your library may have a copy of the ***Guinness Book of World Records.*** First ask students to guess the height of the tallest child in the class. Measure and record the child's actual height. Guess and then measure the height of the teacher. Then using a reference book, ask a pair of students to try to find out the actual recorded height of the world's tallest human and report that information to the class.

With Classroom Teacher Guidance

Sharp-Eye has remarkable vision. Many people wear glasses or contact lenses to improve their eyesight. Students probably have vision testing at school. Invite a local optometrist to visit the school, explain the numbers used to describe eyesight, such as 20/20 and talk about care of the eyes and the use of sunglasses. Be sure students follow up the visit with a thank you note.

Wild Jake Hiccup
The History of America's First Frontiersman
By Sol M. Davidson • Illustrated by Penny Davidson

Summary

The book is divided into sixteen chapters. It relates the life and adventures of Jacob (Wild Jake) Hiccup who was born in a log cabin in western Pennsylvania before the colonies became unified into the United States of America. Wild Jake is so big when he is born, wild animals appear to help nurse the baby.

Jacob's size as a young child causes many problems. Where can he sleep? How can they get enough food for him? How can they cook his oatmeal? What sort of bowls can he use? Each problem is solved in a unique way. Jacob develops hiccups and no remedy seems to cure him, so his parents enter him into a hiccuping contest.

As Jacob grows up, he meets many historical figures. He holds a shoot-out with Daniel Boone, meets up with George Washington and helps him take Fort Duquesne, and serves as a messenger for Samuel Adams. Wild Jake fires the shot heard 'round the world, helps design the American flag, cracks the Liberty Bell, meets up with Davy Crockett and John James Audubon, fights and races against Mike Fink, gets Johnny Apricot-pit started on his way, and finally holds a tremendous fight with Paul Bunyan which ends in a draw.

House of the 9 Muses, 1992. 153 pp. Black and white illustrations. ISBN 1-56412-003-1

Activities

With Librarian Guidance

Have a group of interested students research early flintlock guns in America. They might contact the owner of a local gun shop or antique shop. Information can be found about the Pennsylvania long rifle at **http://www.webpub.com/ ~ jhagee/ky-lr.html**. *The Fighting Handgun: An Illustrated History from the Flintlock to Automatic Weapons,* (Sterling, 1996) would also be informative. Have these students show pictures of the various rifles and share what they learn.

With Classroom Teacher Guidance

1. Have two students research Yellowstone Park's sulphur springs. Are these found elsewhere in the U.S.? The students should write a report on what they learn, complete with a bibliography. They might consult **http://web2.airmail.net/kless/wyoming/yxmas18.htm** and **http://www.nps.gov/yell/**. Two useful books are Marjorie Benson's *Yellowstone* (Raintree Steck-Vaughn, 1995) and David Peterson's *Yellowstone National Park* (Children's Press, 1992.)

2. Ask a small group of students to research and give an oral report on the role of Hessians in the Revolutionary War. They might consult Kathlyn Gay's *Revolutionary War* (Twenty-First Century Books, 1995). A reference library might have *The Hessians and the Other German Auxiliaries of Great Britain in the Revolutionary War*, by Edward Jackson Lowell (Corner House, 1970).

More Resources for Tall Tales

Books

Aylesworth, Jim. *My Sister's Rusty Bike.* Atheneum Books for Young Readers, 1996.

Day, Edward C. *John Tabor's Ride.* Alfred Knopf, 1989.

Dewey, Ariane. *Gib Morgan, Oilman.* Greenwillow Books, 1987.

————. *The Tea Squall.* Greenwillow Books, 1988.

Fleischman, Sid. *McBroom's Wonderful One-Acre Farm.* Greenwillow Books, 1992.

French, Fiona. *Little Inchkin.* Dial Books for Young Readers, 1994.

Grover, Max. *Amazing & Incredible Counting Stories: A Number of Tall Tales.* Browndeer Press, 1995.

Harper, Jo. *Outrageous, Bodacious Boliver Boggs!* Simon & Schuster Books for Young Readers, 1996.

Helldorfer, Mary-Claire. *Moon Trouble.* Bradbury Press, 1994.

Kellogg, Steven. *I Was Born About 10,000 Years Ago: A Tall Tale.* Morrow Junior Books, 1996.

Ketteman, Helen. *Luck With Potatoes.* Orchard Books, 1995.

Mitchell, Adrian. *The Baron All at Sea: More Adventures of Baron Munchausen.* Philomel Books, 1987.

Nolen, Jerdine. *Harvey Potter's Balloon Farm.* Lothrop, Lee & Shepard Books, 1994.

Roth, Susan L. *The Biggest Frog in Australia.* Simon & Schuster Books for Young Readers, 1996.

Slater, Teddy. *The Cow That Could Tap Dance.* Silver Press, 1991.

Spurr, Elizabeth. *The Long, Long, Letter.* Hyperion Books for Children, 1996.

Thompson, Richard. *Cold Night, Brittle Light.* Orca Book Publishers, 1994.

Tunnell, Michael O. *Chinook.* Tambourine Books, 1993.

Van Woerkom, Dorothy. *Tall Corn: A Tall Tale.* Milliken Publishing, 1987.

Wood, Audrey. *The Bunyans.* Blue Sky Press/Scholastic, 1996.

A Short Selected List of Media

Big Annie: An American Tall Tale. Sandra Robbins. See-More Workshop, 1990. 1 book, 32p; 1 sound cassette, 20 min. An American folk tale narrated by Jeff Olmstead.

Ghosts! Alvin Schwartz. HarperCollins, 1995. 1 book, 63p; 1 sound cassette. Includes seven ghost stories based on traditional folktales.

Mose the Fireman. Eric Metaxas. Simon & Schuster, 1996. Rabbit Ears Productions. 1 book (unpaged); 1 sound cassette, 23 min. Tells the tall tale adventures of a nineteenth-century New York fireman.

Pecos Bill. Discis Knowledge Research, 1995. 1 computer laser optical disc. Requires IBM 386 or Mac System 6.0.5. Tales of a legendary American cowboy.

Stormalong. Eric Metaxas. Rabbit Ears Productions, 1995. 1 book, 32p; 1 sound cassette. The legends of a New England sea captain.

Tall Tales & Lost Loot. Robin Snelson. Capstone Entertainment, 1995. 2 videocassettes, 86 min. Includes a guide on the topic of honesty.

Author/Illustrator/Title Index

Subject Index to Major Characters & Activities